MW00679088

What's the Question?

50 Understanding and Thinking Exercises

George E. Mason   **Barbara C. Davis**

J. Weston Walch, Publisher
Portland, Maine

1   2   3   4   5   6   7   8   9   10

ISBN-0-8251-1883-2

Copyright © 1991
J. Weston Walch, Publisher
P.O. Box 658 • Portland, Maine 04104-0658

Printed in the United States of America

Contents

What's the Question? Exercises 1–50

Teacher's Guide

Section I. Introduction and Rationale

Introduction

What's the Question? is a set of fifty exercises for improving the reading comprehension of middle school students. Each exercise consists of a reading passage followed by eight answers with blank lines where students may write questions for which the answers are appropriate. The eight answers are followed by two questions that require students to reason from and/or evaluate the material in the passage. The exercises are graded in difficulty, with the easiest first and most difficult last. The easiest passages are appropriate for students reading at fifth-grade level. The hardest are appropriate for those reading at ninth-grade level or above. The lessons are designed for class instruction, but individualized instruction can easily be developed. (See Section VI.)

Rationale

Research in reading improvement has indicated that teaching self-questioning to students has a positive effect on their comprehension. However, getting students to ask questions is often quite difficult.

Since getting students to develop or create questions does help them comprehend, and since materials for teachers to use for this purpose are scarce, *What's the Question?* was designed to meet those needs.

Providing the answers is one way to ease students into what should become a habit—asking questions as they are reading and using reading to learn the answers. Since the lessons might involve students not only in reading passages and writing questions, but also in reading aloud and listening to the opinions and questions of others, then each lesson can be a whole-language activity involving all four language arts as well as creative and critical thinking.

Section II. Getting Students Ready

Making Sure the Passage Can Be Read

The first lesson for any group of students should be conducted with an exercise based on a passage that is easy for them to read (perhaps Exercise 1). The teacher may discuss the topic (for Exercise 1, it is "The Argument") with students, calling their attention to and clarifying the meanings of any words in the passage that might be difficult. Then the passage may be read by the students.

Observing Student Reading

The teacher should observe students carefully during this reading. If any students are very slow, or if they mumble or read aloud, it might be a good idea for teacher and class to read the passage aloud in unison before using the passage as a vehicle for teaching students to question. When the passage has been read to the teacher's satisfaction, the students are ready to learn to match questions to answers.

Section III. Matching Questions to Answers

Step One

The teacher asks the class to look at the answers listed below the passage. The teacher then reads one of the questions from the Possible Questions in the teacher's guide and asks the class to tell which of the answers matches that question. Discussion then follows. When a consensus has been reached, the teacher is ready for Step Two.

Step Two

The teacher selects one of the answers below the passage and reads aloud three questions from the Possible Questions. The class is asked to choose one of the three as the best question to match the answer. Again students discuss the choices. When they decide, they write the question on the line after the answer. If necessary, the teacher may read the question aloud a second time so that the students may enter it correctly on their exercise sheets.

Step Three

Continue. Read aloud another question from Possible Questions and ask students to match it to one of the answers that appear below the passage. Then, before reading any other questions, ask the students to guess what question might be appropriate for one of the remaining answers. Encourage several students to respond and, if the consensus question corresponds to the question provided, accept the students' stated question. (Note that the wording does not have to be identical.) Have each student write the question on the appropriate line or lines. Complete the exercise in this fashion.

Section IV. Discussing the Bonus Questions

The bonus questions give the teacher the opportunity to help students with questions for which the answer may not be stated in the passage. Many of the questions can be answered through inferential thinking. Some actually have a correct answer. For others, the answer that is considered correct may depend on the answerer's point of view. For questions such as these, one of the teacher's most important tasks is ensuring that all views are heard during the discussions and that students respect the answers of other students whose positions are different from their own.

Section V. Writing Questions Independently

When a class or group of students consistently arrives at appropriate questions through group discussion, the teacher should begin selecting some answers for which students are to write questions independently. The easiest of these are *descriptive questions* (the names of characters or places and the dates or times when events occurred). When most students are able to write descriptive questions (which match the answers given), the teacher may assign the writing of *cause/effect questions*: "Why did something happen?" or "What happened because of this?" If most students are successful in creating cause/effect questions to match the answers given, the teacher may assign the more difficult *process questions*, which request information such as "How do you make a . . . ?" or "How are such things done?"

When students write a question in a blank after discussion has led to a consensus, no further discussion will be needed after the question is written. However, when students have written their questions without any preceding discussion, the teacher should call for oral reading (sharing) of the questions and discuss the merits and demerits of the questions which the class hears individuals read aloud. By so doing, all of the language arts (including listening and speaking) can be enhanced.

Section VI. Providing for Individual Differences

When differences among students in a class are extreme, the teacher may wish to individualize. There are at least three simple methods available:

1. The teacher can create a small group with members who read passages aloud in unison and arrive at questions through oral discussion. Members of the group write their questions after consensus is reached.
2. The teacher can assign less able students to write only descriptive questions (which are easier to compose) before the possible questions are discussed. These students could wait to write in their more complex questions until they have listened to questions written, read aloud, and discussed by the more able students.
3. The teacher can assign easier exercises to poorer readers and harder ones to better readers. (The masters are generally arranged in an ascending order of difficulty: easiest ones first.) When questions are written, all those who have completed the same exercise could meet together as a group to read aloud and discuss the appropriateness of their questions.

Section VII. Motivating Retention of Questioning Skills

A verbal game called "What's the Question?" can be played with the answers and questions in any exercise. The teacher divides the class or group into two or three competing teams. Each team selects one player who will represent the team. Now the game begins.

The teacher reads an answer. Players who think they can state an appropriate question quickly raise their hands. The teacher calls upon the one whose hand was up first and decides whether the question given is acceptable (matches the answer). An acceptable question earns 10 points. If the first question is not accepted, the teacher may call upon a second player who will earn 5 points for an acceptable question. If the second player is unsuccessful, the teacher will allow the third player to consult with his or her team. If the team is able to give its player a correct (acceptable) question, 1 point is awarded to the team. The first team to score 40 or more points is the winner.

Section VIII. Transferring Students' Skills

It is important that students learn to apply their developing reading skills to all of their school texts. Lessons in which students predict the questions that will be found at the end of a chapter in a social studies or science textbook will help accomplish the transfer. Predicting what a mathematics word problem will ask ("What is to be found?") will also be helpful.

Possible Questions for Exercises
and
Suggested Bonus Answers

Exercise 1

1. *Answer:*   Broken glass.
   Question: What did Marcie see on the kitchen floor?

2. *Answer:*   Screams.
   Question: What had Marcie heard a lot of recently?

3. *Answer:*   Hansen.
   Question: What was the last name of Marcie and her parents?

4. *Answer:*   The bedroom.
   Question: From where were the shouts and screams coming?

5. *Answer:*   Hot and thirsty.
   Question: How did Marcie feel when she arrived home from school?

6. *Answer:*   Upstairs.
   Question: Where was Marcie's parents' bedroom?

7. *Answer:*   Two months ago.
   Question: When had Marcie's parents' problems started?

8. *Answer:*   A business trip.
   Question: What had taken Marcie's father to New Orleans?

Bonus Answers

A. Accept students' statements and encourage them to speculate as to whether Marcie's father or mother is the glass-breaker.

B. This topic is eminently worthy of discussion. Accept all positions.

Exercise 2

1. *Answer:*   "Johnson the Jerk."
   Question: Who lost a contract for Bob Hansen's company?

2. *Answer:*   18 years.
   Question: How long had the Hansens been married?

3. *Answer:*   Six o'clock.
   Question: When were Bob Hansen's meals ready?

4. *Answer:*   Marcie.
   Question: Who was listening outside her parents' bedroom door?

5. *Answer:*   New Orleans.
   Question: Where had Bob Hansen gone on his business trip?

6. *Answer:*   A good wife.
   Question: What had Ann Hansen been?

7. *Answer:*   Upstairs.
   Question: Where was Mr. and Mrs. Hansen's bedroom?

8. *Answer:*   A bleached blonde.
   Question: Of whom was Ann Hansen jealous?

Bonus Answers

A. Accept students' answers and encourage discussion. Allow teams to write position papers.

B. Remind students that they may be married in a few years, perhaps fewer than five. Help them understand the importance of communication between marriage partners.

Exercise 3

1. *Answer:*   Bob Hansen and Julia Jarrard.
   Question: Who went on the trip to New Orleans?

2. *Answer:*   Three.
   Question: How many husbands had Julia had?

3. *Answer:*   Number Four.
   Question: What did Ann Hansen say that Bob Hansen was going to be?

4. *Answer:*   The bedroom.
   Question: Where were Bob and Ann arguing?

5. *Answer:*   Ann Hansen's friend.
   Question: Who told Ann about Bob Hansen's night life in New Orleans?

6. *Answer:*   Night spots along the shore.
   Question: Where had Ann's friend said that she had seen Bob and Julia?

7. *Answer:*   Staring at the open door.
   Question: What was Ann Hansen doing when Marcie entered the bedroom?

8. *Answer:*   A suitcase.
   Question: What was Bob Hansen carrying with him when we went down the stairs?

Bonus Answers

A. One of the answers which should be accepted is "Nothing." However, accept all answers and elicit as much discussion as possible. It could be therapeutic for some students.

B. Encourage argument and oral reading from the passage to support positions taken.

C. This is a good chance to make two points: (1) that a person should be considered innocent until proven guilty, and (2) that sometimes friends shouldn't tell friends everything. You may wish to engage the students in a discussion of whether Ann's friend should have told Ann about what she saw in New Orleans.

Exercise 4

1. *Answer:*   An abandoned church.
   Question: Where were Joey and Marty to meet the club members to join the club?

2. *Answer:*   Standing in a circle.
   Question: How were the members arranged when Joey and Marty met them at the church?

3. *Answer:*   Chuck Black.
   Question: Who was the club's president?/Whom did Joey ask about joining?

4. *Answer:*   Get in the middle of the circle.
   Question: What did Chuck's voice tell Joey and Marty to do?

5. *Answer:*   Halloween.
   Question: When was "new members night"?

6. *Answer:*   Joey.
   Question: Which boy had first heard about the club?

7. *Answer:*   Three weeks earlier.
   Question: When had Joey first heard about the club?

8. *Answer:*   Black hoods.
   Question: What were the club members all wearing at the church?

Bonus Answers

A. During discussion, help students understand the connotation as well as the derivation of the word *abandoned.*

B. Help students understand that anonymity emboldens the wearers of masks and frightens others, who are faced with unfamiliar and therefore threatening beings.

Exercise 5

1. *Answer:*   Dead meat.
   Question: What did Dusty say he was?

2. *Answer:*   Between the shoulders.
   Question: Where had Joshua hit Dusty?

3. *Answer:*   The art teacher.
   Question: Who was Mrs. Brown?

4. *Answer:*   In the hall at school.
   Question: Where was Dusty when Joshua whacked him?/Where was Joshua when Dusty hit him back?

5. *Answer:*   The lady at the desk.
   Question: To whom did Dusty give the note?/Who told him to be seated?

6. *Answer:*   Mrs. Brown.
    Question: Who wrote the note to the principal?

7. *Answer:*   Nervous.
    Question: What was Dusty like when he waited for Mr. Patterson to see him?

8. *Answer:*   Joshua.
    Question: Who had whacked Dusty?/Who got a bloody nose?

Bonus Answers

A. Encourage discussion of rights and responsibilities. Elicit the qualities of good citizenship.

B. Accept students' answers and encourage discussion. You may wish to group students into teams to write position papers.

Exercise 6

1. *Answer:*   Mr. Patterson.
    Question: Who was the principal?

2. *Answer:*   In the nose.
    Question: Where did Dusty hit the other student?

3. *Answer:*   The lady at the desk.
    Question: Who told Dusty that he could go into the principal's office?

4. *Answer:*   Dusty's father.
    Question: Who would the principal call if Dusty decided not to do what the principal asked him to do?

5. *Answer:*   Not serious.
    Question: What did Dusty think about the principal's request when he first heard it?

6. *Answer:*   Glass.
    Question: What sort of top was on the principal's desk?

7. *Answer:*   A small ant.
    Question: What did Dusty feel like as he sat across the desk from the principal?

8. *Answer:*   Behind a desk.
    Question: Where did the principal sit?

Bonus Answers

A. Accept all reasonable answers. Help the class decide which are most reasonable and which may be unlikely.

B. Encourage discussion about the various types of punishments parents and teachers may legally exact.

Exercise 7

1. *Answer:*   Joey.
   Question: Who was the person who stole the ring?

2. *Answer:*   Bret.
   Question: Who took the jewelry?

3. *Answer:*   Garbage cans.
   Question: What were the boys hiding behind?

4. *Answer:*   A used car.
   Question: For what did Bret want money?

5. *Answer:*   Blackburn's jewelry store.
   Question: What store had Bret stolen from?

6. *Answer:*   A ring.
   Question: What did Bret steal?

7. *Answer:*   A pawn shop.
   Question: Where did Bret want to take the ring?

8. *Answer:*   Toliver.
   Question: Where was the pawn shop?

Bonus Answers

A. Accept students' responses. Encourage discussion that uses recall of details from the passage to support reasons for choosing ages.

B. In order to answer this question, you may need the help of a lawyer or judge. Joey is certainly guilty of a crime if he helps Bret dispose of the jewelry, but just running with Bret might not be a crime if Joey could get a judge to believe him. You might assign two or three students to take the passage to a lawyer or judge (or make phone calls) in order to get an opinion. You also might invite a lawyer or judge to your classroom to be interviewed by your students.

Exercise 8

1. *Answer:*   Nervous and angry.
   Question: How did Joey feel after the theft?

2. *Answer:*   Blackburn.
   Question: Who was waiting on customers in the store?

3. *Answer:*   Silverware.
   Question: What had the girl in the store been looking at when Bret stole the ring?

4. *Answer:*   Baby blue.
   Question: What color will Bret paint the convertible that he plans to buy?

5. *Answer:*   Ten years.
   Question: How long does Joey think they'll spend behind bars if they're caught?

6. *Answer:*   Moran's store.
   Question: What store had the boys broken into six months earlier?

7. *Answer:*   A convertible.
   Question: What did Bret want to buy with the money he could get for the stolen ring?

8. *Answer:*   Officer Beatty.
   Question: Who caught the boys?

Bonus Answers

A. Accept any reasonable answer. Encourage students to consider all avenues of communication.

B. Encourage students to discuss friendship and what it means and doesn't mean.

Exercise 9

1. *Answer:*   Mark.
   Question: Who is Tonya's boyfriend?

2. *Answer:*   A letter jacket.
   Question: What was Mark wearing?

3. *Answer:*   A drug overdose.
   Question: What did the other students think caused Mark to pass out?

4. *Answer:*   Mr. Henderson.
   Question: Who is the principal of the school?

5. *Answer:*   Students with bad reputations.
   Question: With whom had Mark been hanging around?

6. *Answer:*   Acting strangely and repeating phrases.
   Question: What had Mark been doing that morning?

7. *Answer:*   Worried and frightened.
   Question: How did Tonya feel when she heard someone say that the person on the floor was Mark?

8. *Answer:*   Sprawled out on the floor in the hall at school.
   Question: Where is Mark?

Bonus Answers

A. Accept any logical explanation. If necessary, suggest diabetes, epilepsy, walking pneumonia, a blow to the head, or choking (toothpick chewing is a major cause of choking).

B. Elicit as many different positions as possible and encourage students to seek to understand why others prefer different courses of action in emergency situations.

Exercise 10

1. *Answer:*   She knelt and used her flashlight to look into Mark's eye.
   Question: What did the nurse do when she arrived?

2. *Answer:*   Tonya.
   Question: Who was Mark's girlfriend who begged to stay near him?

3. *Answer:*   Her stethoscope.
   Question: What did Mrs. Folet use to listen to Mark's heart?

4. *Answer:*   He ran toward his office to call an ambulance.
   Question: What did Mr. Henderson do?

5. *Answer:*   Two football coaches.
   Question: Who carried Mark to the nurse's office?

6. *Answer:*   Mrs. Folet.
   Question: Who was the school nurse?

7. *Answer:*   The ambulance.
   Question: What whisked Mark away?

8. *Answer:*   He looked nearly dead.
   Question: How did Mark look to Tonya?

Bonus Answers

A. Mrs. Folet probably would not have sent for an ambulance if Mark were dead, but this could have encouraged or discouraged Tonya. Elicit student discussion of both possibilities.

B. Help the students to understand that she could still hear Mark's heartbeat with the stethoscope, even though his pulse may have been too weak to feel.

Exercise 11

1. *Answer:*   All summer.
   Question: How long had Beth been trying to get over being angry at Lisa?

2. *Answer:*   In the garage.
   Question: Where was the Studebaker?

3. *Answer:*   An old car.
   Question: What is a Studebaker?

4. *Answer:*   Beth's father.
   Question: Who was restoring the old Studebaker?

5. *Answer:*   Beth's mother.
   Question: Who walked over to Beth with her head bowed?

6. *Answer:*   She had been crying.
   Question: What had Beth's mother been doing before she walked over to Beth with her head bowed?

7. *Answer:*   Ruling the household.
   Question: What did Beth think Lisa was doing?

8. *Answer:*   Beth's sister.
   Question: Who is Lisa?

Bonus Answers

A. Something that her parents had kept Beth from knowing. (Accept students' guesses.)

B. Encourage students to discuss such sensitive topics as (1) being adopted, (2) having a relative who may be dying, and (3) having a relative who is an alcoholic or drug addict.

Exercise 12

1. *Answer:*   Honey.
   Question: What does Beth's mother call Beth?

2. *Answer:*   Less than a year.
   Question: How long will Lisa live?

3. *Answer:*   He is the one who found the tumor.
   Question: Who is the doctor?

4. *Answer:*   She has a tumor. She is Beth's older sister.
   Question: Who is Lisa?

5. *Answer:*   She is Lisa's sister.
   Question: Who is Beth?

6. *Answer:*   She was sorry.
   Question: How did Beth feel when she found out about Lisa's tumor?

7. *Answer:*   It was not Beth's fault.
   Question: What did Beth's mother say about Beth's babyish behavior?

8. *Answer:*   A brain tumor.
   Question: What is killing Lisa?

Bonus Answers

A. Accept students' answers and encourage a discussion of their reasons.

B. Students should be able to use the context of the sentence to derive this meaning. Also, analysis of the prefix *in* (not), *opera* (work), and *able* (capable of being) should be encouraged as a means of deriving the meaning of this word. It means "cannot be operated on."

Exercise 13

1. *Answer:*   One year.
   Question: How long had Karen and Danny been dating?

2. *Answer:*   Fabulously.
   Question: How had they gotten along at first?

3. *Answer:*   Watch TV at her house.
   Question: What did they do on their dates lately?

4. *Answer:*   Danny's behavior.
   Question: What did Karen try to excuse?

5. *Answer:*   Preoccupied.
   Question: How did Danny look when he came to Karen's house on Friday?

6. *Answer:*   He did not love her anymore.
   Question: What did Danny tell her?

7. *Answer:*   Confused; lonely.
   Question: How did Karen feel about Danny after he left?

8. *Answer:*   Depressed.
   Question: What kind of mood would you say Karen was in?

Bonus Answers

A. Accept all answers, encouraging students to draw inferences from their own experiences.

B. Be sure that students consider a number of possibilities, including the possibility that Danny was on drugs.

Exercise 14

1. *Answer:*   Receivers.
   Question: Who was running away from the defenders?

2. *Answer:*   A cinch.
   Question: What did people think the Dragons' chances of winning were?

3. *Answer:*   65 percent.
   Question: What was the quarterback's passing record so far?

4. *Answer:*   Logged.
   Question: What word means that they kept track of the number of interceptions?

5. *Answer:*   Fantastic speeds.
   Question: What speeds could be run by Albermarle's receivers?

6. *Answer:*   Rivals.
   Question: Who were the Blue Devils?/What is Canton?

7. *Answer:*   44.
   Question: What was Russ's number?/Who was everyone watching?

8. *Answer:*   28–14.
   Question: What was the score at halftime?

Bonus Answers

A. Answers should indicate that *key* means essential. Help students draw the analogy between *key block* and a key essential for unlocking a locked door.

B. Accept any reasonable answer—teacher, coach, relative, friend. Encourage discussion about storytellers and their tales.

Exercise 15

1. *Answer:*   Six.
   Question: With only two minutes left to play, how many points ahead of the Blue Devils were the Dragons?

2. *Answer:*   94 yards.
   Question: How long was the Blue Devils' final touchdown run?

3. *Answer:*   Roberts.
   Question: Who threw the ball to Russ?/Who was the Dragons' quarterback?

4. *Answer:*   Clinch.
   Question: What word means make sure of?

5. *Answer:*   Perfect.
   Question: What kind of pass did Roberts throw?

6. *Answer:*   Two field goals.
   Question: What had put the Dragons up by six points?

7. *Answer:*   A substitute.
   Question: Who scored the last touchdown for the Blue Devils?

8. *Answer:*   Good.
   Question: What was the point-after-touchdown (p.a.t.)?

Bonus Answers

A. Allow students to reread the passage to find the words *goat* and *never be able to show his face in Albermarle again.* Discuss what *face* means in various cultures.

B. Encourage discussion and elicit statements not only about what Russ should do, but also about what his friends should do. You might wish to assign individuals the task of writing notes to Russ to help him feel better.

Exercise 16

1. *Answer:*   A cruiser.
   Question: What kind of ship was the U.S.S. *Indianapolis?*

2. *Answer:*   Nearly 1,200.
   Question: How many men were on the *Indianapolis* when it was torpedoed?

3. *Answer:*   Nearly 900.
   Question: How many men died when their ship sank?

4. *Answer:*   The U.S.S. *Cecil J. Doyle.*
   Question: What ship rescued Morgan and the other men on his raft?

5. *Answer:*   An American sailor.
   Question: Who was Glenn Morgan?

6. *Answer:*   Japanese torpedoes.
   Question: What hit and sank the *Indianapolis?*

7. *Answer:*   A big shark.
   Question: Who was Charlie?

8. *Answer:*   Five days.
   Question: How long did the survivors drift before they were picked up?

Bonus Answers

A. Students can infer Glenn's birth date by subtracting his age (21) from the year of the sinking (1945).

B. Students should infer that cruisers are named after cities.

Exercise 17

1. *Answer:*   66 feet.
   Question: What is the distance between wickets on a cricket field?

2. *Answer:*   In the crease.
   Question: When a batsman is ready to bat, where do cricket players say that he is?

3. *Answer:*   A batsman.
   Question: What is the batter called?

4. *Answer:*   Eleven.
   Question: How many players are on a cricket team?

5. *Answer:*   Bowler.
   Question: Who throws or rolls the ball to begin play?

6. *Answer:*   Six.
   Question: How many runs are scored if the batsman hits the ball out of the playing area on the fly?

7. *Answer:*   Four.
   Question: How many runs are scored if the batsman hits the ball out of the playing area on one bounce?

8. *Answer:*   Ten.
   Question: How many outs end an innings?

Bonus Answers

A. Accept logical answers, including *runs, outs, catcher.*

B. Outfielders and designated batters are good guesses. Have students give reasons for their answers.

Exercise 18

1. *Answer:*   Touching up her lipliner.
   Question: What was the lady trying to do when she gave her lips green edges?

2. *Answer:*   Mrs. Dracula.
   Question: Who did the lady look like, at first?

3. *Answer:*   Red with green edges.
   Question: What color were the lady's lips when Charlie first looked in his mirror?

4. *Answer:*   The bus driver.
   Question: Who was Charlie?

5. *Answer:*   White leather.
   Question: What kind of purse did the lady carry?

6. *Answer:*   A little handkerchief.
   Question: What did the lady use to scrub her lips?

7. *Answer:*   ". . . once might have been white."
   Question: What words tell that the stuff on the lady's lips was coming off on the handkerchief?

8. *Answer:*   Pink.
   Question: What color did the lady's lips turn as she scrubbed them?

Bonus Answers

A. Students should infer that her handkerchief would have been white, red, and green.

B. Help students with the inference that since she couldn't see in the dark, she guessed by the feel of her eyeliner. It must have felt like her lipliner.

Exercise 19

1. *Answer:*   Jack.
   Question: Who went through the ice into the pond?

2. *Answer:*   Fall and winter.
   Question: When does this story take place?

3. *Answer:*   Oak.
   Question: What kind of tree held the tree house?

4. *Answer:*   In Brian's backyard.
   Question: Where was the big oak tree with the tree house in it?

5. *Answer:*   In back of Thompson's shed.
   Question: Where did Brian see the old sled?

6. *Answer:*   A hammer, a wrecking bar, and a rope.
   Question: What equipment did Brian think would be needed for tearing down the tree house?

7. *Answer:*   His hero.
   Question: What had Jack called Brian after Brian pulled him out of the pond?

8. *Answer:*   Morrison's Pond.
   Question: Where was the ice that Jack went through?

Bonus Answers

A. Help students infer that Brian meant the fall or the football season.

B. Accept students' answers and encourage them to make inferences based on their own experiences.

Exercise 20

1. *Answer:*   A peaceful place.
   Question: What was the tree house?

2. *Answer:*   He built the tree house.
   Question: Who was Brian?/What did Brian do long ago?

3. *Answer:*   It was burying a bone.
   Question: What was Laura's Irish setter doing?

4. *Answer:*   Stalking something.
   Question: What was Ol' Dan doing?

5. *Answer:*   Laughter.
   Question: What could Brian hear from down below?

6. *Answer:*   Ten or eleven.
   Question: How old had Brian been when he was last in the tree house?

7. *Answer:*   Brian's mother.
   Question: Who insisted that the tree house come down?

8. *Answer:*   Muffled.
   Question: How did the children's voices sound to Brian?

Bonus Answers

A. Help students to infer that because it was winter, the leaves were off the trees.

B. Encourage students to think of the "pretend" games they played as children and to include imagination as one of the things Brian used when he had played in the tree house.

Exercise 21

1. *Answer:*   The old mansion.
   Question: Where did Gram live?/What frightened Marla?

2. *Answer:*   Marla.
   Question: Who was Gram's great-granddaughter?/Who was afraid of the mansion?

3. *Answer:*   Gram.
   Question: Who was Marla's great-grandmother?/Who was pale?/Who was lying in bed?

4. *Answer:*   The west wing.
   Question: Where did Gram and her husband live when they first married?

5. *Answer:*   Deep in her chest.
   Question: From where were Gram's sounds coming?

6. *Answer:*   Gram's mumbling.
   Question: What didn't make sense?

7. *Answer:*   A weeping willow.
   Question: What hung over the east balcony?

8. *Answer:*   Night.
   Question: What time of day does the story take place?

Bonus Answers

A. Help students to infer that the oak was the tallest tree.

B. Help students to infer that Marla had to live close enough so that she could either walk or take a short drive to the mansion.

Exercise 22

1. *Answer:*   Gram's name.
   Question: What is Clarissa?

2. *Answer:*   Incoherently.
   Question: How (in what way) was Gram whispering?

3. *Answer:*   Charles.
   Question: Who was Gram's husband?

4. *Answer:*   Nine.
   Question: What time was it when the clock struck?

5. *Answer:*   A smile.
   Question: What was on Gram's lips?

6. *Answer:*   Peaceful.
   Question: How did Marla feel after the light rose from Gram's body?

7. *Answer:*   A quilt.
   Question: With what did Marla cover Gram?

8. *Answer:*   Across her chest.
   Question: Where were Gram's arms?

Bonus Answers

A. Help students infer that it was the anniversary of the wedding of Charles and Clarissa.

B. Accept students' answers. Be sure that one of the questions they raise is "Who wrote the note?"

Exercise 23

1. *Answer:* The city's lights all went out.
   Question: What had happened simultaneously?

2. *Answer:* He intended to calm them.
   Question: Why did Harrison go to his neighbor's house?

3. *Answer:* In the bedroom.
   Question: Where was Harrison's flashlight?

4. *Answer:* The mother of two small children.
   Question: Who was Mrs. Johnson?

5. *Answer:* Next door to Harrison.
   Question: Where did the Johnsons live?

6. *Answer:* Violent.
   Question: What word tells you that it was a bad storm?

7. *Answer:* His flashlight.
   Question: What did Harrison give the woman?

8. *Answer:* To stay inside.
   Question: What did the woman promise to do?

Bonus Answers

A. There are a number of possible answers, including "The Blackout," "A Strange Night," "An Unexplainable Force."

B. Encourage students' predictions; elicit reasons for their predictions.

Exercise 24

1. *Answer:* Eerie.
   Question: What kind of feeling is in the air during the storm?

2. *Answer:* It means to get inside his own house.
   Question: What does it mean to hurry "to the shelter of his own roof"?

3. *Answer:* Cratzoidanian.
   Question: What sort of "lovely dinner" were the aliens going to have?/What word describes where the aliens were from?

4. *Answer:* He was approaching his house.
   Question: Where was Harrison when his candles and lantern went out?

5. *Answer:* He panicked and moved to the right and to the left.
   Question: What did Harrison do when he couldn't find the door?

6. *Answer:* Tremendous knives.
   Question: What did the Cratzoidanians have in their hands?

7. *Answer:*   He passed out.
   Question: What happened when "darkness overcame him"?

8. *Answer:*   In a room filled with strange lights.
   Question: Where was Harrison when he awoke?

Bonus Answers

A. Accept students' views. Those who believe that life exists on other planets and that aliens visit Earth will state that it could have happened. Those who deny that aliens from outer space visit Earth will state that this story could not have happened.

B. Answers will vary. Encourage students to express creative answers. Taking dictation and writing a group response to complete the story would be an excellent teaching strategy.

Exercise 25

1. *Answer:*   Rocking Texas roadhouse blues.
   Question: What was Stevie Ray Vaughan's musical style?

2. *Answer:*   In a helicopter crash.
   Question: How did Stevie Ray Vaughan die?

3. *Answer:*   In late August, 1990.
   Question: When did Stevie Ray Vaughan die?

4. *Answer:*   Dallas, Texas.
   Question: Where was Stevie Ray Vaughan born?

5. *Answer:*   He couldn't get drugs.
   Question: Why did Stevie Ray stay drunk in London?

6. *Answer:*   The music of B.B. King and Muddy Waters.
   Question: Whose music was Stevie Ray's music most like?

7. *Answer:*   *Couldn't Stand the Weather.*
   Question: What was Stevie Ray's 1984 platinum record?

8. *Answer:*   Stevie Ray collapsed.
   Question: What happened to Stevie Ray in London?

Bonus Answers

A. Encourage students to discuss the many ways in which people express grief.

B. Be sure students understand the short-term highs and the long-term debilitating effects of alcohol and other drugs. It seems likely that he would have died from alcohol or drugs if he hadn't discontinued his use of them. He probably would not have been a star.

Exercise 26

1. *Answer:*   Late fall.
   Question: When were Corey and Stephanie married?

2. *Answer:*   Rob.
   Question: Who was killed in an auto accident?

3. *Answer:*   Dreams and disappointments.
   Question: What did Stephanie and Corey share?

4. *Answer:*   In Stephanie's backyard.
   Question: Where was the wedding held?

5. *Answer:*   To the slide.
   Question: Where was Corey going when he knocked Stephanie down?

6. *Answer:*   Corey.
   Question: What is the name of Stephanie's boyfriend?

7. *Answer:*   A lifetime.
   Question: How long did the young couple think their love would last?

8. *Answer:*   Kindergarten.
   Question: Where had Stephanie met Corey?

Bonus Answers

A. Encourage discussion of, and help students appreciate, the ways authors develop backgrounds for stories before launching into their plots.

B. Be sure students note that only Stephanie's thoughts and words are presented.

Exercise 27

1. *Answer:*   Fishing trawlers' nets.
   Question: What kills the most giant sea turtles?

2. *Answer:*   Turtle-exclusion devices.
   Question: What can shrimp boats put on their nets to save the sea turtles?

3. *Answer:*   120.
   Question: How many mother sea turtles nested on Cumberland Island in 1964?

4. *Answer:*   Three.
   Question: At least how many years go by before the mother turtle returns?

5. *Answer:*   Four or five times.
   Question: How many times will the mother turtle lay eggs in one summer?

6. *Answer:*   One foot.
   Question: How deep does a mother turtle dig her nest?

7. *Answer:*   One every 10 seconds.
   Question: How fast does she lay her eggs?

8. *Answer:*   24.
   Question: How many loggerheads laid eggs on Cumberland Island in 1989?

Bonus Answers

A. 96. If students cannot get this answer, show that this answer results from subtracting the 1989 number (24) from the 1964 number (120).

Bonus Answers

B. Encourage students to reason that the turtle-exclusion devices will cost fisherman extra money and that some resentment is to be expected.

Exercise 28

1. *Answer:*   Jefferson High School.
   Question: Where did Molly go to school?

2. *Answer:*   In her mother's car.
   Question: How did Molly ride to school?

3. *Answer:*   Molly's skirt.
   Question: What was shut in the car door?

4. *Answer:*   Spanish.
   Question: Into what classroom did Molly think she was going?

5. *Answer:*   Greek mythology.
   Question: What was the class lecture about?

6. *Answer:*   Report her absent.
   Question: What didn't Molly want her Spanish teacher to do?

7. *Answer:*   Tiptoed to the door.
   Question: How did Molly leave the lecture on mythology?

8. *Answer:*   Snicker and whisper.
   Question: What did Molly hear other students do?

Bonus Answers

A. Accept all answers and ask students to explain their hypotheses.

B. Have students justify their predictions by citing their own experiences and the experiences of others they have known.

Exercise 29

1. *Answer:*   Mike.
   Question: What is short for microphone?

2. *Answer:*   Jefferson High School.
   Question: Where does this story take place?/What is the setting?

3. *Answer:*   Josh Desmond.
   Question: Who caught Molly's retainer?

4. *Answer:*   The Student Council.
   Question: What meeting had Molly attended?/To what had Molly been elected?/What was the school's student government called?

5. *Answer:*   Rarely.
   Question: How often was a newcomer elected to the Student Council?

6. *Answer:*   A gorgeous guy.
   Question: Who was Josh Desmond?

7. *Answer:*   Her tongue stuck to it.
   Question: Why did the retainer fly out of Molly's mouth?

8. *Answer:*   Glowing.
   Question: What word means that Molly felt wonderful?

Bonus Answers

A. Help students to infer that, because this event occurred in the school parking lot, many people must have witnessed it and found it amusing.

B. Encourage students to infer that Molly's mouth was very dry. Discuss other symptoms of fear with the class or group: tremors, sweaty palms, tense muscles, etc.

Exercise 30

1. *Answer:*   Topps.
   Question: What company had a monopoly on baseball cards from 1955 to 1980 and is still the only company that can give out cards with bubble gum?

2. *Answer:*   Five cents.
   Question: How much did the early cards cost?

3. *Answer:* $24 or more.
   Question: How much does a complete set of baseball cards from one manufacturer cost today?

4. *Answer:*   Tobacco companies.
   Question: What companies were the first to give away baseball cards with their products?

5. *Answer:*   Honus Wagner.
   Question: What card sold for $100,000?

6. *Answer:* $5,000.
   Question: How much is a Mickey Mantle rookie card in mint condition worth?

7. *Answer:*   A monopoly.
   Question: What did Topps have with regard to the baseball card market from 1955 to 1980?

8. *Answer:*   In mint condition.
   Question: What term means that the cards are still like new?

Bonus Answers

A. Help students understand that the first cards were made to help sell tobacco and gum, but that now the cards themselves are moneymakers. Also lead them to understand that more people will lose money than make money.

B. Accept students' estimates and encourage speculation on the worth of particular cards they (or one of their friends or relatives) may possess.

Exercise 31

1. *Answer:*   Little kisses.
   Question: What does Crystal give Jackie?

2. *Answer:*   150.
   Question: How many members are in the American Fancy Rat and Mouse Association in southern California?

3. *Answer:*   The English.
   Question: Who were the first people to make pets of rats?

4. *Answer:* $10.
   Question: How much does a really fine rat cost?

5. *Answer:*   *Rat and Mouse Tales.*
   Question: What is the association newsletter called?

6. *Answer:*   Twice a month.
   Question: How often is *Rat and Mouse Tales* printed?

7. *Answer:*   Jackie Jennings.
   Question: Who is Crystal's owner?/Who is vice president of the American Fancy Rat and Mouse Association?

8. *Answer:*   Crystal.
   Question: What is Jackie Jennings' rat named?

Bonus Answers

A. Accept all students' answers. Elicit maximum discussion. List pros and cons of rat ownership on the chalkboard.

B. Encourage students to consider how others might react if they heard a rat's squeaking coming from Jackie's purse as she walked through a store or restaurant.

Exercise 32

1. *Answer:*   Cape Canaveral.
   Question: From where did the NASA shuttle ship *Discovery* blast off?

2. *Answer:*   *Ulysses.*
   Question: What satellite did the *Discovery* crew start toward the sun?

3. *Answer:*   Five years.
   Question: How long will it take *Ulysses* to reach the sun?

4. *Answer:*   93 million miles.
   Question: How far is the trip from the earth to the sun?

5. *Answer:*   Thousands of miles per hour.
   Question: How fast is *Ulysses* moving?

6. *Answer:*   *Discovery.*
   Question: What spaceship fired off the *Ulysses* satellite?

7. *Answer:*   Edwards Air Force Base.
   Question: Where did *Discovery* land after sending off the satellite *Ulysses?*

8. *Answer:*   6:57 A.M., October 9, 1990.
   Question: When did *Discovery* land at Edwards Air Force Base?

Bonus Answers

A. Help students understand that great speed is necessary to leave Earth's orbit and that such speed is easier to obtain by firing satellites from space shuttles.

B. Help students solve this distance, rate, and time problem. If the trip will take five years, how many days will it take? How many hours? Divide 93 million by that number of hours and you'll have the approximate speed of the satellite.

Exercise 33

1. *Answer:*   The third man to break the five-second barrier.
   Question: Who is Richard Holcombe?

2. *Answer:*   Holcombe's time for the run.
   Question: What is 4.99 seconds?

3. *Answer:*   The clutch on the spare engine.
   Question: What hadn't been set properly?

4. *Answer:*   Wichita Falls, Texas.
   Question: Where was Eddie Hill from?

5. *Answer:*   Gene Snow.
   Question: Which of the other record-holders was from Fort Worth?

6. *Answer:*   The Chief Auto Parts Nationals.
   Question: What races were being run when Holcombe broke the five-second barrier?

7. *Answer:*   The International Hot Rod Association.
   Question: Who sponsored the races Holcombe had entered?

8. *Answer:*   Holcombe's fastest speed ever.
   Question: What is 277.89 miles per hour?

Bonus Answers

A. Accept reasonable answers: It was the only other engine they had; they were desperate; someone thought that it might not be worn out; etc.

B. Accept all reasonable answers. Encourage students to explain their reasons.

Exercise 34

1. *Answer:*   True mental anguish.
   Question: What is clinical depression?

2. *Answer:*   Nearly 10 percent.
   Question: What proportion of American men suffer from depression?

3. *Answer:*   More than 20 percent.
   Question: What proportion of American women suffer from depression?

4. *Answer:*   Antidepressant drugs, talk therapy, psychoanalysis, shock therapy.
   Question: What treatments for depression are available?

5. *Answer:*   A psychiatrist from Bethesda, Maryland.
   Question: Who is Harold Eist?

6. *Answer:*   Famous people who suffered from depression.
   Question: Who were Abraham Lincoln and Winston Churchill?

7. *Answer:*   20 million.
   Question: How many Americans may be afflicted with depression?

8. *Answer:*   Dysthymia.
   Question: What is a mild form of depression?

Bonus Answers

A. Helps student to infer that attempts at suicide might be symptoms of clinical depression.

B. Accept all answers, and encourage students to offer reasons for the answers given.

Exercise 35

1. *Answer:*   Not great at first.
   Question: What is the pay for a young pilot?

2. *Answer:*   Fly with an instructor.
   Question: What must one do before soloing?

3. *Answer:*   Chief pilot and manager of a big flight school.
   Question: Who is Clint Rodgers?

4. *Answer:*   Young people.
   Question: Who are hoping to make flying a career?

5. *Answer:*   Between $2,500 and $4,000.
   Question: What does it usually cost to learn to fly in a flight school?

6. *Answer:*   Check-ride.
   Question: What must the student perform with an examiner on board before being licensed?

7. *Answer:*   35 hours.
   Question: What amount of ground school instruction is required?

8. *Answer:*   A regional airline.
   Question: Where might a young pilot get started on a flying job?

Bonus Answers

A. Ask students to name the airlines they have heard about. Then classify these as local, regional, national, or international airlines.

B. Help students infer the answers by adding the 35 hours of flying to the 35 in ground school.

Exercise 36

1. *Answer:*   Frank Hoffman.
   Question: Who was injured and in Intensive Care?

2. *Answer:*   An automobile accident.
   Question: How had Chad been killed and Frank injured?

3. *Answer:*   Chad Montgomery.
   Question: Who had been killed?

4. *Answer:*   Jefferson County High School.
   Question: Where had Chad and Frank been students?

5. *Answer:*   Two years.
   Question: How long had Chad been dating his girlfriend?

6. *Answer:*   Quarterback.
   Question: What position had Chad played on the football team?

7. *Answer:*   Melanie.
   Question: Who was Chad's girlfriend?

8. *Answer:*   The junior-senior prom.
   Question: What dance was coming up the next week?

Bonus Answers

A. Help students understand the need to learn the facts before assigning blame. If none of them points it out, remind them that in the United States a person is presumed innocent until proven guilty.

B. Accept students' answers and probe for their reasons. Ask what their ages might have been and discuss the responsibilities of marriage.

Exercise 37

1. *Answer:*   Nine lives.
   Question: What don't cats have?

2. *Answer:*   Daressa Hooper.
   Question: Who is Shadow's owner?

3. *Answer:*   Madison, Wisconsin.
   Question: Where does Boogs live?

4. *Answer:*   A six-year-old cat.
   Question: What is Boogs?

5. *Answer:*   37 days.
   Question: How long was Shadow missing?

6. *Answer:*   Grey and white.
   Question: What color is Boogs?

7. *Answer:*   A state judge.
   Question: Who ruled that Boogs would not die?

8. *Answer:*   Grafton, Virginia.
   Question: Where does Shadow live?

Bonus Answers

A. Accept students' estimates, encouraging them to guess that Shadow was inside fewer than 37 days.

B. Encourage speculation. Be sure students consider the possibility that water was in the bottom of the machine.

Exercise 38

1. *Answer:*   Roanoke Island.
   Question: Where was the first English colony in the New World?

2. *Answer:*   Two.
   Question: How many pregnant women were among the settlers?

3. *Answer:*   John White.
   Question: Who was the leader and the appointed governor of the colony?

4. *Answer:*   John White's daugher, a pregnant woman.
   Question: Who was Elenor Dare?

5. *Answer:*   1587.
   Question: When was the Lost Colony founded?

6. *Answer:*   The first English child born in America.
   Question: Who was Virginia Dare?

7. *Answer:*   To fight the Spanish Armada.
   Question: Why did England need all of its ships in 1587 and 1588?

8. *Answer:*   Hatteras Island.
   Question: Where was Croatoan?/What is Croatoan?

Bonus Answers

A. After students have given their opinions, encourage them to do library research to find the explanations offered by historians.

B. Be sure students understand that in Colonial times ocean travel was as hazardous as colonizing the new lands. Accept each student's view and list reasons.

Exercise 39

1. *Answer:*   Poisonous, nonpoisonous, constrictive.
   Question: What are the three types of snakes?

2. *Answer:*   North Pole, South Pole, some ocean islands.
   Question: Where don't snakes live?

3. *Answer:*   Venom.
   Question: What does a poisonous snake inject into its prey?

4. *Answer:*   Squeezes it.
   Question: How does a constrictor kill its prey?

5. *Answer:*   Embedded in their bodies.
   Question: Where are tiny legs found in pythons and boas?

6. *Answer:*   Elastic ligaments.
   Question: How are a snake's jaws connected?

7. *Answer:*   Its jaws open wide.
   Question: How can a snake swallow prey much larger than itself?

8. *Answer:*   Digestive enzymes.
   Question: What dissolves the prey so that it can be absorbed into the snake's bloodstream?

Bonus Answers

A. Accept all plausible answers, especially cold areas and inaccessible islands. Encourage students to check out their guesses using reference works. (Examples include Antarctica, Iceland, Ireland, Greenland.)

B. Accept students' opinions. Be sure that they have noted, however, that the snakes' scales press *against irregularities* in the surface beneath them in order for the snake to move.

Exercise 40

1. *Answer:*   Thousands of teenagers.
   Question: Who have been forced into armies?

2. *Answer:*   Ten years.
   Question: For how long had forced recruiting been the custom in El Salvador?

3. *Answer:*   Violeta Chamarro.
   Question: Who was the president of Nicaragua in 1990?

4. *Answer:*   Draft notices.
   Question: What did young men in El Salvador ignore?

5. *Answer:*   They picketed their president.
   Question: What did high school students in Honduras do?

6. *Answer:*   At bus stops.
   Question: Where had students been waiting when the Honduran army recruited them by force?

7. *Answer:*   The draft ended.
   Question: Why were Nicaraguan students smiling and moving around freely in 1990?

8. *Answer:*   200,000.
   Question: How many soldiers under the age of fifteen were fighting in wars in 1990?

Bonus Answers

A. Help students to infer that the ropes had been around the new recruits.

B. Accept students' answers and elicit their reasons. You may wish to set up a formal debate on this question.

Exercise 41

1. *Answer:*   Light Amplified Stimulated Emission of Radiation.
   Question: What is a laser?

2. *Answer:*   The same as the flash of light that started it.
   Question: What is the wavelength of the rays in a laser beam?

3. *Answer:*   Ordinary light rays.
   Question: What spread out and travel in in all directions?

4. *Answer:*   Rays in a laser beam.
   Question: What move in the same direction and all have the same wavelength?

5. *Answer:*   They have the same wavelength.
   Question: Why are rays of laser beams all one color?

6. *Answer:*   Each crest is lined up with the crests of the other rays.
   Question: Why are laser beams so powerful?

7. *Answer:*   Different wavelengths.
   Question: What makes ordinary light consist of many colors?

8. *Answer:*   Just one.
   Question: How many wavelengths are in the waves from the beam that is used to start a laser beam?

Bonus Answers

A. Help students infer that they grow weaker, because they spread out farther and farther as they travel through space.

B. Help students infer that a laser printer burns the letters onto the paper.

Exercise 42

1. *Answer:*   Wheelbarrows and broomsticks.
   Question: What did one general call the old weapons and equipment that Guard members had used in the past?

2. *Answer:*   Melvin Laird.
   Question: Who was the secretary of defense in 1978?

3. *Answer:*   39.
   Question: How many days per year did Guard members train before 1978?

4. *Answer:*   67.
   Question: How many days on the average do Guard members now train each year?

5. *Answer:*   100.
   Question: How many days might a National Guard commander have to spend in training each year?

6. *Answer:*   South Carolina.
   Question: What state was battered by Hurricane Hugo?

7. *Answer:*   The governor of South Carolina.
   Question: Who called up 7,200 Guard members to help victims of Hurricane Hugo?

8. *Answer:*   Total Force.
   Question: What did Secretary of Defense Laird call his plan that called for the National Guard to be better trained?

Bonus Answers

A. Accept answers appropriate to your area of the country. Be sure that the following three are included: citizen soldiers, weekend warriors, patriots.

B. Accept any logical answer. Among others, elicit the following: (1) They are needed for defense. (2) The best training is at a far-off location.

Exercise 43

1. *Answer:*   "The Panda Bears."
   Question: What was the second squadron called?/In what squadron was Jim Howard?

2. *Answer:*   Claire Lee Chenneault.
   Question: Who commanded "The Flying Tigers"?

3. *Answer:*   "Hell's Angels."
   Question: What was the third squadron called?/In what squadron was Parker Dupuoy?

4. *Answer:*   Over Germany.
   Question: Jim Howard won the Congressional Medal of Honor for aerial combat over which country?

5. *Answer:*   America's highest award.
   Question: What is the Congressional Medal of Honor?

6. *Answer:*   Aerial combat.
   Question: What is fighting in airplanes called?

7. *Answer:*   A toothy snarl.
   Question: What was painted on the nose of each P-40?

8. *Answer:*   China and Burma.
   Question: Where did "The Flying Tigers" fight?

Bonus Answers

A. The first squadron. If students cannot infer this answer, help them find the names of the second and third squadrons and then ask who Adam and Eve were.

B. Accept answers that could be possible: The Americans wanted adventure or excitement; they loved to fly; they favored China; they opposed Japan; etc.

Exercise 44

1. *Answer:*   Carbon dioxide.
   Question: What do trees take in (that we breathe out)?

2. *Answer:*   Provide a thermostat that helps to regulate it.
   Question: What do trees do for the earth's temperature?

3. *Answer:*   The rain forests.
   Question: What actually creates rain?

4. *Answer:*   Green umbrellas.
   Question: What does the author call the leafy treetops?

5. *Answer:*   Masterpieces of nature.
   Question: What are trees?

6. *Answer:*   On the snow.
   Question: Where do trees cast lovely dark images?

7. *Answer:*   Noxious.
   Question: What word means harmful to our health?

8. *Answer:*   Evergreens.
   Question: What trees provide color in the winter?

Bonus Answers

A. Help students use context to infer that it means to replace or put back.

B. Encourage students to air their views about the warming of the earth and the impact of the loss of our rain forests on the earth's climate.

Exercise 45

1. *Answer:*   The Cherokee version.
   Question: What version of toli is very rough?

2. *Answer:*   Little baskets on the ends of their sticks.
   Question: What do toli players use to catch and throw the ball?

3. *Answer:*   Toli.
   Question: What ancient game is played with sticks that have little baskets on the ends?

4. *Answer:*   By touching or hitting the goal pole with the ball.
   Question: How are points scored?

5. *Answer:*   A team.
   Question: What is made of 25 players?

6. *Answer:*   The Choctaw version.
   Question: Which version of toli is played most often today?

7. *Answer:*   Two.
   Question: How many sticks does each toli player carry?

8. *Answer:*   The goal pole.
   Question: What is 12 feet tall?/What must be hit or touched for a score to occur?

Bonus Answers

A. Encourage students to use reference works to find the rules of jai alai and lacrosse and to research how they are played. Then the two can be compared to toli.

B. Accept students' answers, making sure they understand that the Cherokee version is very rough and dangerous.

Exercise 46

1. *Answer:*   Sophisticated equipment.
   Question: What did the pioneers lack?

2. *Answer:*   The animals' fur was thick.
   Question: What might cause settlers to predict a cold winter?

3. *Answer:*   A reliable prediction.
   Question: What was "Red sky in the morning, sailors take warning!"?

4. *Answer:*   They guessed wrong.
   Question: What might have caused their crops to be lost or their animals to freeze?

5. *Answer:*   Weather folklore.
   Question: What was part of a pioneer's eduction?

6. *Answer:*   Pioneers and settlers.
   Question: What early Americans are mentioned in this passage?

7. *Answer:*   Olfactory sense.
   Question: What is one's sense of smell?

8. *Answer:*   The meteorologist.
   Question: Who predicts the weather today?

Bonus Answers

A. Accept students' answers and encourage their explanations.

B. Write students' responses on the chalkboard. After several responses have been written, conduct a discussion until a consensus title is achieved. Here are some possibilities: "Weather Forecasting"; "Weather Folklore"; "Pioneer Weather Forecasting"; "Meteorology: Old and New."

Exercise 47

1. *Answer:*   The C.S.S. *Alabama.*
   Question: What was the most notorious Confederate battleship?

2. *Answer:*   Abraham Lincoln.
   Question: Who called the C.S.S. *Alabama* "a pirate ship"?

3. *Answer:*   James Dunwoody Bulloch.
   Question: Who designed the C.S.S. *Alabama*?

4. *Answer:*   Raphael Semmes.
   Question: Who was the captain of the C.S.S. *Alabama*?

5. *Answer:*   Mobile, Alabama.
   Question: Where was the captain from?

6. *Answer:*   England.
   Question: Where were most of the crew members from?

7. *Answer:*   Union merchant ships.
   Question: What kinds of ships did the C.S.S. *Alabama* attack?

8. *Answer:*   Its "watery death."
   Question: What words does the author use to tell that the ship sank?

Bonus Answers

A. Help students infer that since the remains had not yet been raised, Watts must have seen the ship under the sea off the coast of France.

B. Point out that *H.M.S.* on British ships stands for "Her Majesty's Ship" and that *U.S.S.* stands for "United States Ship." This should enable students to infer that *C.S.S.* stands for "Confederate States Ship."

Exercise 48

1. *Answer:*   The United States.
   Question: To whom did France give the remains of the C.S.S. *Alabama*?

2. *Answer:*   Columbus, Georgia.
   Question: Where is the Confederate Naval Museum?

3. *Answer:* A confederate battleship.
   Question: What was the C.S.S. *Alabama?*

4. *Answer:* France's.
   Question: In those waters was the C.S.S. *Alabama* found?

5. *Answer:* England.
   Question: Where was the C.S.S. *Alabama* constructed?/From what country did most of its crew members come?

6. *Answer:* An archaeologist from East Carolina University.
   Question: Who was Dr. Watts?

7. *Answer:* The only museum in the world devoted exclusively to the Confederate Navy.
   Question: What is the Confederate Naval Museum?

8. *Answer:* Captain Semmes.
   Question: Who was a native of Alabama?

Bonus Answers

A. Encourage students to describe each of the points that indicate the value of the find. If time permits, list them on the chalkboard as they are brought out.

B. Tell students to pretend that they are a committee assembled to decide where the ship will go. Ask for volunteers to represent each of the competing groups.

Exercise 49

1. *Answer:* The U.S. Patent Office.
   Question: What organization turned Morse down at first when he applied for a patent?

2. *Answer:* Morse applied for a patent.
   Question: What did Samuel Morse do in 1837?

3. *Answer:* He studied art there.
   Question: What did Morse do in London?

4. *Answer:* 1832.
   Question: When did Morse develop his plan for the telegraph?

5. *Answer:* Charleston, Massachusetts.
   Question: Where was Morse born?

6. *Answer:* New Haven, Connecticut.
   Question: Where did Morse work from 1832 unitl 1837?

7. *Answer:* The first message sent by telegraph.
   Question: What is "What hath God wrought!"?

8. *Answer:* May 18, 1844.
   Question: When was the first telegraph message sent?

Bonus Answers

A. Students can infer the year (1851) by adding seven to the year of the first message (1844).

B. Students can infer Morse's age when he worked out his plan by subtracting his date of birth (1791) from the year in which he worked out the plan (1832).

Exercise 50

1. *Answer:*   A singing group that has been together for thirty years.
   Question: Who are The Impressions?

2. *Answer:*   "For Your Precious Love."
   Question: What was the first big hit by the Impressions?

3. *Answer:*   It made it to number 4.
   Question: What is "It's All Right"?

4. *Answer:*   He said, "Music is constantly changing . . ."
   Question: Who is Fred Cash?

5. *Answer:*   The Roosters.
   Question: What was the first name The Impressions used?

6. *Answer:*   Pride and unity among black people.
   Question: What messages did The Impressions' music carry?

7. *Answer:*   Fred Cash, Sam Gooden, Ralph Johnson, Vandy Hampton.
   Question: Who are the members of The Impressions?

8. *Answer:*   More than 20 million.
   Question: How many of The Impressions' records have been sold?

Bonus Answers

A. Students may infer the answer by subtracting the Top-40 records (seventeen) from their "more than fifty" total. The answer is, of course, "more than thirty-three."

B. Accept the students' own opinions and elicit the reasons for those opinions.

What's the Question?

Marcie ran up the steps to her door. It was a terribly hot afternoon and she had walked home from school. The long, hot walk had made her extremely thirsty. She opened the door and went into the kitchen. There she headed straight for the refrigerator. Suddenly she stopped. There was broken glass on the floor! Knives, forks, and pans had been tossed around! This worried Marcie. Her mother was a very neat person. She usually kept everything spotless. Marcie stopped and listened. Her heart was beating very fast.

From upstairs came voices. It sounded like an argument. There were shouts and curses! It was awful!

This was not the first time she had heard sounds of this sort. They usually came from her parents' bedroom. Lately, screams were a part of daily life. The Hansen household was troubled.

Marcie didn't know what was going on. Her mom and dad had never had problems until about two months ago. That was when her father had returned from a business trip to New Orleans. It seemed to start then. After that, her mother and father argued constantly. Yet they wouldn't discuss matters with Marcie. All they told her was that they had some things to "iron out." They said that everything would soon be all right. Marcie wondered if "everything" would *ever* be all right!

The Answers

1. Broken glass. _____

2. Screams. _____

3. Hansen. _____

4. The bedroom. _____

5. Hot and thirsty. _____

6. Upstairs. _____

7. Two months ago. _____

8. A business trip. _____

Bonus Questions

A. What do you think is causing the broken glass on the kitchen floor and the screaming upstairs in Marcie's house?

_____

B. When parents are having difficulty getting along with each other, should they explain their disagreements to their children? Explain your position.

_____

What's the Question?

Marcie stole quietly up the stairs. She stopped outside the door of her parents' room. She had to listen. There were screams and threats coming from within.

"How could you have done this to me?" shouted Mrs. Hansen. "For eighteen years I've kept your house clean. I've raised our children. I've done the very best I know how. Your meals have always been on the table at six o'clock. I even got your paper!"

"Ann, I *know* you've been a good wife. You don't have to keep reminding me of it! Don't you think I get a little tired of hearing about it? Don't you think I ever do anything for *you*?"

"Oh, I know about all you do for me. You go to work every day. You sit across the room from some bleached blonde. You make eyes at her all day. And the very first chance you get, you're off to New Orleans with her. That's what you do for me!" Ann Hansen had started crying.

"I told you it was a business trip," said Bob Hansen. He was clenching his teeth. "Can't you get that through your skull? We went to New Orleans to try to get a contract. 'Johnson the Jerk' had lost it for us!"

The Answers

1. "Johnson the Jerk." _____

2. 18 years. _____

3. Six o'clock. _____

4. Marcie. _____

5. New Orleans. _____

6. A good wife. _____

7. Upstairs. _____

8. A bleached blonde. _____

Bonus Questions

A. Should Marcie have listened at her parents' bedroom door? Why or why not?

_____

B. Is the fact that more women are working causing more marriages to break up? What can be done to help people save their marriages?

_____

What's the Question?

Name _____

Date _____

"I told you it was a business trip!" said Bob Hansen. He was clenching his teeth. "Can't you get that through your skull? We went to New Orleans to try to get a contract. 'Johnson the Jerk' had lost it for us! It was nothing more than that!"

"Well, I don't believe you," Ann Hansen answered. "Ms. Julia Jarrard has been after you for a long time. And don't tell me you haven't noticed. She's already had three husbands. Now she's looking for Number Four. Well, it looks like you're going to be it! I *know* about New Orleans, Bob. A friend of mine was there when you were. She told me about the moonlight strolls. She told me about Julia. She told me about the little dinners for two. She said that the two of you hit all the night spots along the shore! Let me ask you one question, John. When did you start kissing her goodnight?"

Marcie didn't hear anything more from the bedroom. She stood still and waited. She hoped her father had some excuse. But before she knew it, he rushed out of the room. He brushed past her without a word. Then he went down the stairs. He was carrying a suitcase with him. Marcie went into the bedroom. She found her mother sitting on the bed. Ann was staring at the open door.

The Answers

1. Bob Hansen and Julia Jarrard. _____

2. Three. _____

3. Number Four. _____

4. The bedroom. _____

5. Ann Hansen's friend. _____

6. Night spots along the shore. _____

_____

7. Staring at the open door. _____

8. A suitcase. _____

Bonus Questions

A. What should Marcie say to Ann? Why?

_____

B. Do you think Bob Hansen had been unfaithful? Or was he just angry that his wife didn't trust him? Explain your position.

_____

C. Suppose Ann's friend was not telling the truth. What should Marcie do?

_____

What's the Question?

It had started three weeks earlier. Joey had heard about a new club. He and Marty decided to check it out. They found that a lot of guys were in it. Marty and Joey wanted to get in it, too.

Chuck Black was the club's president. Joey asked him about joining. Chuck just grinned. The way he looked made Joey feel funny. Then Chuck said, "Sure, man. Just be ready on Halloween night. We're having 'new members night.' We'll let you join us then."

Joey and Marty really were excited. They made plans about which girls they would call after they became members.

At last Halloween night came. The two boys met the club members at an old abandoned church. The members were standing in a circle. They all had on black hoods with holes for their eyes and mouths. Chuck's voice came from one of the hoods. It told Joey and Marty to get into the middle of the circle. The two boys began to sweat.

The Answers

1. An abandoned church. _____

2. Standing in a circle. _____

3. Chuck Black. _____

4. Get in the middle of the circle. _____
   _____

5. Halloween. _____

6. Joey. _____

7. Three weeks earlier. _____

8. Black hoods. _____

Bonus Questions

A. What are some reasons why the club chose the abandoned church for their "new members night"?
   _____

B. Why do members of some clubs wear masks when they are taking in new members? What purpose do the masks serve?
   _____

What's the Question?

Name _____

Date _____

"Dusty, this is the last straw! Wait right here. I'm going to write a note to the principal. You are going to see Mr. Patterson." Mrs. Brown, the art teacher, was not fooling.

"Oh, no!" thought Dusty. "My dad's going to kill me! He told me that if I was sent to the office, he would see that I never go out again. I'm dead meat!"

Dusty made his way to Mr. Patterson's office. He had the horrible note in his hand. He didn't even understand how everything had come about. There he was, just standing in the hall. Joshua had walked up behind him and whacked him between the shoulders.

All Dusty did was turn around and punch Joshua in the nose. So, it bled a little. Well, maybe more than a little. Okay, it bled a lot. Well, what did they expect him to do? Just stand there and take it? "Well, I'm just not made that way," thought Dusty. "I'm not gonna let some punk pick on me. They'll just have to understand that."

Dusty gave his note to the lady at the desk. She told him to be seated. Mr. Patterson would be right with him. He sat there, getting more and more nervous. What was Mr. Patterson like? What was going to happen to him?

The Answers

1. Dead meat. _____

2. Between the shoulders. _____

3. The art teacher. _____

4. In the hall at school. _____

5. The lady at the desk. _____

6. Mrs. Brown. _____

7. Nervous. _____

8. Joshua. _____

Bonus Questions

A. When someone hits you, should you hit back? Why or why not? Suppose you were not in school when you got hit. Would your answer be different?

_____

B. Should parents punish children again when they have already been punished at school? Explain your position.

_____

What's the Question?

Name _____

Date _____

Dusty waited forever. Finally, the lady at the desk called him. She told him to go into Mr. Patterson's office.

Mr. Patterson sat behind a big desk. Dusty sat down. He could just see the man. Only his head showed above the glass desktop. Mr. Patterson glared at him. Dusty felt like a small ant about to be eaten by an anteater.

"Well, young man," began the principal. "What is this all about?"

"Uh, sir, I guess I just didn't think. I forgot what I was doing," answered Dusty.

"You punched a fellow student in the nose. Giving someone a nosebleed is very serious, you know. If Mrs. Brown had not come along, there would have been a real fight."

"I'm sorry," said Dusty. His voice was very low.

"Well, I want to make sure that this never happens again," Mr. Patterson went on. "Here's what I want you to do."

Dusty listened to Mr. Patterson. He couldn't believe what the man said. Surely the man wasn't serious! Surely he didn't want Dusty to do *that*!

"What do you say, Dusty?" asked the principal. "Are you willing to do it? If you are, we'll forget this whole thing. If not, I'll just give your father a call. He may have some suggestions about how to handle this."

The Answers

1. Mr. Patterson. _____

2. In the nose. _____

3. The lady at the desk. _____

4. Dusty's father. _____

5. Not serious. _____

6. Glass. _____

7. A small ant. _____

8. Behind a desk. _____

Bonus Questions

A. What do you think the principal wanted Dusty to do? Why was Dusty shocked by the request?

_____

B. If you were Dusty, would you do what the principal asked (if it was not immoral or illegal), or would you let him call your father? Why?

_____

What's the Question?

Name _____

Date _____

"Hey, man, why did you go and do that?" asked Joey. He was out of breath. They had run all the way from Blackburn's jewelry store. Now they were making their way down an alley.

"Here!" whispered Bret. "Let's hide behind these barrels for a while. These big barrels will hide us until the coast is clear."

"Bret, I can't believe you took that ring. You said we were just going to look. I never would have gone in with you if I had known you'd *steal* something!" Joey was shaking behind the garbage can. He didn't even notice the foul odor.

"I didn't plan it, man," answered Bret. "I got the idea while we were inside. Think about the money we can get for this ring. We can buy Old Man Meadows's used car. He wants $2,000 for it, and we can get at least that for this piece of ice!"

"Where will you sell it, smart guy? Blackburn's is the only jewelry store in town, and they're not going to buy back a ring some punk stole from them." Joey spoke softly, but strongly.

"We can take it to Toliver. There's a pawn shop there. We can pretend we got it from our poor dying grandmother," suggested Bret.

The boys had calmed down somewhat. They began to notice the stench from the garbage cans. It was strong! But they continued to nestle behind them. It had been several minutes since they left the jewelry store. Bret leaned his head back against the brick wall of the alley.

The Answers

1. Joey. _____

2. Bret. _____

3. Garbage cans. _____

4. A used car. _____

5. Blackburn's jewelry store. _____

6. A ring. _____

7. A pawn shop. _____

8. Toliver. _____

Bonus Questions

A. How old are the two boys? Why do you think so?

_____

B. Should Joey report the crime to the authorities? Is he guilty of a crime? Why or why not?

_____

What's the Question?

Name _____

Date _____

Joey was shocked. Bret had stolen a diamond ring while they were in a jewelry store. They both ran as soon as they were out of the store. Now they were hiding in an alley behind some big garbage cans.

"Don't look at me that way, man! Nobody's going to know. Nobody saw me. Blackburn was helping that girl who was looking at the silverware. As soon as he turned his back, I pocketed it. He didn't see a thing. Man, you think I'm a real dope! Well, I'll show you. I'm going to be driving around in a cool convertible. You know what I'm going to do, Joey? I'm going to paint it baby blue. Then I'll put a new top on it. White, I think. Won't that look great?" Bret was trying to calm Joey. Joey was nervous and angry.

"Bret, if I get in trouble, it'll be your fault! Who cares about a dumb old convertible? How are you going to drive it when you're behind bars? They're going to lock us away for ten years! The tires will be rotted off when we get out." Joey was really worried. He had tried to do everything right since they got caught breaking into Moran's store six months ago. He knew another rap would mean time in jail.

Suddenly, the boys heard a sound. Looking up, they saw a policeman's cap. Then Officer Beatty stepped around the trash can.

"Okay, boys," he said. "Hand over the ring."

"Yes, sir," said Bret. "I was just telling Joey he had to take it back."

"Bret!" gasped Joey.

The Answers

1. Nervous and angry. _____

2. Blackburn. _____

3. Silverware. _____

4. Baby blue. _____

5. Ten years. _____

6. Moran's store. _____

7. A convertible. _____

8. Officer Beatty. _____

Bonus Questions

A. How do you think Officer Beatty learned that a ring had been stolen? How did he know where to look for the boys?

_____

B. What is Bret trying to do to Joey? What should Joey do?

_____

What's the Question?

Name _____

Date _____

"Who is it?" asked Tonya. She was pushing her way through the crowd in the hall. She had heard that some kid had passed out. People thought it was probably an overdose of drugs. She was trying to find out who it was.

"Beats me," said one of the other students.

"Somebody said it was Mark," said another. "I saw him fall, but I couldn't see who it was. I did see that he had on a letter jacket. That's all I could see. Everybody ran out of the classroom right after he went down. I couldn't see him after that."

Tonya was really worried. Mark was her boyfriend. He had acted strangely that morning, and she had wondered why. He kept repeating phrases again and again. Lately, Mark had been hanging around with a tough group. The group had a bad reputation. Could he be on drugs?

Tonya was trying to press her way through the students. They had gathered around to see whoever was lying on the floor. "Please let me through!" she begged. Her heart was beating faster every moment. What if it was Mark? Maybe she should have notified someone. He had been acting very strangely. She kept trying to get through, but it was hard. Everyone else was trying to see. No one would move out of the way.

Finally Mr. Henderson, the principal, arrived on the scene. He demanded that everyone get back to class. Gradually the hall cleared. Now Tonya could clearly see the young man in the letter jacket. It was Mark, sprawled out on the floor.

The Answers

1. Mark. _____

2. A letter jacket. _____

3. A drug overdose. _____

4. Mr. Henderson. _____

5. Students with bad reputations. _____

6. Acting strangely and repeating phrases. _____

   _____

7. Worried and frightened. _____

8. Sprawled out on the floor in the hall at school. _____

   _____

Bonus Questions

A. Name three or more things that might have happened to Mark. Which do you think is most likely? Why?

   _____

B. What should Tonya do? Why?

   _____

What's the Question?

At last the other students went to their rooms. The principal had made them leave. Now Tonya could see what they had been looking at. When Tonya saw that it was Mark sprawled out on the floor, she knelt down and turned his head so that she could see his face. Mr. Henderson told her that she had to go on to class, but she begged him to let her stay. He finally agreed that she could stay until the nurse got there, but told her that then she would have to leave.

Mrs. Folet, the school nurse, came running down the hall and knelt by Mark. She took out her small flashlight, peeled back an eyelid, and looked into Mark's eye. She felt for a pulse and then looked at her watch. Then she took out her stethoscope and listened to Mark's heart. Calmly, she told Mr. Henderson to call for an ambulance and to notify Mark's parents.

Mr. Henderson ran for the office. He had forgotten to remind Tonya to go back to class, so she stood by, looking on in horror. Mark hardly looked alive! What was wrong with him? Why hadn't she been more concerned about him earlier? Maybe this never would have happened if she had told someone Mark had been acting funny.

In a few minutes, Mr. Henderson returned with two of the football coaches. Mark hadn't moved, but Tonya could see that he was breathing. Following Mrs. Folet's instructions, they moved Mark to the nurse's office and laid him on the bed. Tonya followed them and watched Mark through the office window until the ambulance arrived and whisked him away.

The Answers

1. She knelt and used her flashlight to look into Mark's eye. _____

2. Tonya. _____

3. Her stethoscope. _____

4. He ran toward his office to call an ambulance. _____

5. Two football coaches. _____

6. Mrs. Folet. _____

7. The ambulance. _____

8. He looked nearly dead. _____

Bonus Questions

A. Should Tonya have been encouraged when Mrs. Folet told the principal to call for an ambulance? Why?

_____

B. Why did Mrs. Folet use her stethoscope after feeling for Mark's pulse?

_____

What's the Question?

"It's just not right, Mom. Lisa gets all the attention around here, and nobody even knows I exist. All I asked was to watch my very favorite television program, and no, Lisa has to watch something else. Well, why does she always get her way about everything? Why is she so much more important than I am? Tell me that!"

Beth stormed out of the house and went to the garage to sit for a while and try to get over her anger. It seemed as if she had spent all summer trying to get over her anger toward Lisa. What was going on, anyway? Why was everyone bowing down to Lisa? When did she start ruling the household?

Beth was sitting in the back seat of the old Studebaker that her father was restoring when she heard someone come into the garage. She looked up. It was her mother. Mrs. Arnold walked over to Beth with her head bowed, and when she looked up, Beth could tell she had been crying.

"What is it, Mom?" she asked.

"Beth, I didn't realize until just now that we've done you a terrible injustice. I want to explain some things to you. I think then that your feelings toward your sister will change a little."

Beth had no idea what her mother was about to say, but she felt it was really serious. What in the world could be wrong? What was this "injustice" that her mother was talking about?

"Beth, your dad and I were trying to keep you from hurting so much, but now we realize that in keeping this from you, we hurt you even more."

"Keeping *what* from me, Mom?"

The Answers

1. All summer. _____

2. In the garage. _____

3. An old car. _____

4. Beth's father. _____

5. Beth's mother. _____

6. She had been crying. _____

7. Ruling the household. _____

8. Beth's sister. _____

Bonus Questions

A. What was the terrible injustice?

_____

B. Should parents tell their children everything or should they hold back some information? If they should hold back, what kinds of information should they keep from their children? Why?

_____

What's the Question?

Name _____

Date _____

Beth was really upset with her mother and father for pampering her older sister. She felt jealousy and resentment toward her sister. Then her mother came to her and explained, "Honey, your sister is very ill. She probably won't live another year. The doctor found a tumor on her brain. That's why she was having all of those headaches a few weeks ago.

"The tumor is inoperable; we just have to leave it alone and watch it slowly kill her. She's taking medication; the doctor put her on it when I took her to the clinic. It lessens the pain, but it makes her awfully sleepy. Have you noticed how she sleeps so much lately? Beth, I . . . "

"Oh, Mom! Oh, Mom! It's going to be all right! I wish you had told me about this before, Mom, but I understand. I'm sorry I've been acting like such a baby. I've put more on you and Dad than you already had. I'm sorry, Mom."

"Honey, it's not your fault. I'm glad you know, though. Maybe we can help each other now. I really am going to need you now. I don't think I can make it without you."

"Mom, I'll be here whenever you need me. Let's just go and see if we can do something for Lisa now." Beth and her mother walked out of the garage with their arms around each other.

The Answers

1. Honey. _____

2. Less than a year. _____

3. He is the one who found the tumor. _____

4. She has a tumor. She is Beth's older sister. _____

5. She is Lisa's sister. _____

6. She was sorry. _____

7. It was not Beth's fault. _____

8. A brain tumor. _____

Bonus Questions

A. Should Beth have been jealous of her sister?

_____

B. What is the meaning of *inoperable*?

_____

What's the Question?

Name _____

Date _____

The wind blew lazily through the trees as Karen sat looking longingly out the window. Just last night she had watched out that window as Danny drove away for the last time. Karen couldn't figure out what had happened.

She and Danny had been going together for a year. They had gotten along fabulously until about a month ago. Then she started noticing that something had changed. Danny was quieter, and he never wanted to go out. Lately they had spent all of their time at her house watching TV. And often Danny would call at the last minute, saying that something had come up and he couldn't come.

Karen had told herself that nothing was wrong. She made excuses for Danny's behavior. He wasn't feeling well; maybe he was worried; maybe he was getting low grades; maybe his parents were separating. But last night she learned the truth.

When Danny came to her house for their usual Friday evening date, he looked so preoccupied that Karen asked what was on his mind. At first Danny didn't want to talk about it, but then he told her that he simply did not love her anymore. He wanted to date other girls. He said he hoped she understood.

Karen didn't understand! She got up from the sofa and went to her room and shut the door. Danny let himself out, and she watched from her window as he drove away. She sat there all night, crying, and when morning came she was still wondering what in the world had gone wrong and how she would ever live without him.

The Answers

1. One year. _____

2. Fabulously. _____

3. Watch TV at her house. _____

4. Danny's behavior. _____

5. Preoccupied. _____

6. He did not love her anymore. _____

7. Confused; lonely. _____

8. Depressed. _____

Bonus Questions

A. Why do you suppose Danny decided that he didn't love Karen anymore?

_____

B. If Danny still loved Karen, what other explanation might be given for his change of behavior?

_____

EXERCISE 14:

What's the Question?

Name _____

Date _____

I suppose if Russ had even dreamed of what might happen on that night, he would have stayed at home and faked a stomachache. But as it was, the night of the "big game" was here—the game the entire school had been waiting for all year. Russ was expected to lead the team to victory against Albermarle's biggest rival, the Blue Devils of Canton. Russ's stomach didn't feel too steady that night, but it wasn't a virus or anything like that. It was simply an outright case of the nervous jitters, the kind of feeling that made one want to get on with the action, to go ahead and show everyone who the real champs were.

It was a cinch that the Dragons were going to bury the Blue Devils. All season long the Dragons could do no wrong. Their quarterback was completing 65 percent of his passes, and the receivers were running away from the defenders at fantastic speeds. Their ground game was almost perfect, and when it wasn't, their runners could find holes where holes didn't exist. Their defense hardly ever let anyone through, and they had logged more interceptions this year than in the last five years combined. What a team!

At halftime, this night had been no different. Russ had run for two touchdowns, and had thrown key blocks for the other two that Albermarle had made. Both teams had kicked and made all their extra points. Russ's team was two touchdowns ahead and his own name was called over the loudspeaker so many times that even those who were not from Albermarle soon knew that Number 44 was *The Man*.

The Answers

1. Receivers. _____

2. A cinch. _____

3. 65 percent. _____

4. Logged. _____

5. Fantastic speeds. _____

6. Rivals. _____

7. 44. _____

8. 28–14. _____

Bonus Questions

A. What is a *key block*? Why is the word *key* used by the author?

_____

B. Who do you think is telling this story? Who says "I suppose" at its beginning?

_____

What's the Question?

Name _____

Date _____

It was fourth quarter; two minutes to go! The Blue Devils were giving it all they had, but the Albermarle Dragons had kicked two field goals to go ahead by six and were threatening to score again. Albermarle had the ball on the Canton eight-yard line, first down. Roberts took the ball from center and dropped back to pass. Russ faked a block, then sneaked into the end zone, turned, and waited for the pass that would clinch the victory. Roberts threw. The crowd was on its feet, yelling, screaming. The pass was perfect, straight as an arrow to its target, and Russ waited in perfect position all alone in the end zone.

No one could explain what happened next. The ball went straight into Russ's hands—and right on through them! The Canton fans went wild; the Albermarle fans could not believe their eyes. The Blue Devils took heart. They stopped the next three plays for a net of only two yards, and when they regained possession, a substitute running back raced down the sidelines for a 94-yard touchdown. The point-after-touchdown was good; the Blue Devils had won by one point, and instead of being a hero, Russ was a goat. He'd never be able to show his face in Albermarle again.

The Answers

1. Six. _____

2. 94 yards. _____

3. Roberts. _____

4. Clinch. _____

5. Perfect. _____

6. Two field goals. _____

7. A substitute. _____

8. Good. _____

Bonus Questions

A. What words mean that Russ couldn't meet his friends without feeling terrible?

_____

B. What should Russ do on Monday? Should he go to school or stay home?

_____

What's the Question?

Name _____

Date _____

Glenn Morgan, a twenty-one-year-old American sailor, had just finished his watch. It was July 30, 1945, and he was on the bridge of the U.S.S. *Indianapolis* when Japanese torpedoes hit. "When I hit the water, I swam away. I'd always heard the sinking ship would suck you under," he said.

Morgan grabbed a rubber tube and watched in the moonlight. The ship was gone in twelve minutes! With its propellers still turning as its stern raised above the South Pacific waves, the big cruiser plunged to the bottom. Nearly 900 sleeping U.S. sailors were lost; only about 300 survived.

Glenn Morgan survived because he swam to a big rubber raft and crawled into it with twenty other survivors. The raft had rations, kegs of water, and a first-aid kit. Nevertheless, one man died. He had been burned badly and needed more than first aid.

For the next five days, the raft drifted. The Navy didn't search for the survivors at first, because the *Indianapolis* had been unable to send out a "Mayday" before it sank.

The men on the raft fished and watched a huge shark that they named Charlie. Every time the men would finish a can of food, they'd throw it overboard. Almost immediately, Charlie would be seen swimming around the raft. Once the huge shark raised his head and lunged halfway into the raft. But no one was hurt and Charlie backed off without taking any of the men with him.

Although no one was looking for the survivors, a U.S. plane on patrol did spot them. Soon ships were searching for them. After five days afloat on the raft, Glenn Morgan climbed aboard the destroyer U.S.S. *Cecil J. Doyle*. "Those big blue searchlights certainly looked good to me," Morgan said. "Oh, how good they looked!"

The Answers

1. A cruiser. _____

2. Nearly 1,200. _____

3. Nearly 900. _____

4. The U.S.S. *Cecil J. Doyle*. _____

5. An American sailor. _____

6. Japanese torpedoes. _____

7. A big shark. _____

8. Five days. _____

Bonus Questions

A. When was Glenn Morgan born?

_____

B. How are the U.S. cruisers named?

_____

What's the Question?

Name _____

Date _____

Cricket is played on a rectangular field that's up to 550 feet on each side. It takes about 30 minutes to set up the playing field. First the two wickets must be set up near the center of the field, 66 feet apart. A wicket is three poles, 20 inches high, with two cross bars close enough together so the ball can't get through. The batsman stands in front of the wicket and the bowler throws or rolls the ball toward it. The batsman tries to hit the ball to keep it from reaching the wicket. When the batsman is ready to bat, he's "in the crease."

If the batsman hits the ball out of the playing field on the fly, he scores six runs. It he hits it out on one bounce, he scores four runs. One run is scored if a new batsman replaces the previous batsman before that man is out. An innings lasts until all 11 men have scored or until there are 10 outs. Often a team will score more than 100 runs in one innings, and games sometimes last all day or go on for several days.

If the bowler gets the ball past the batsman and it hits the wicket, the batsman's turn is ended. If the batsman steps out of the crease and a fielder hits the wicket with the ball, the batsman is also through. And if the catcher strikes the wicket while holding the ball, the batsman is "stumped," which means he's out. If the batsman blocks the ball with his body or if he uses his hands to keep the ball away from the wicket, he is also out.

The Answers

1. 66 feet. _____

2. In the crease. _____

3. A batsman. _____

4. Eleven. _____

5. Bowler. _____

6. Six. _____

7. Four. _____

8. Ten. _____

Bonus Questions

A. What words are used in both cricket and baseball?

_____

B. Which baseball players might make the best cricket batsmen?

_____

   What's the Question?

What's the Question?

Charlie didn't believe what he heard, but he looked at the inside mirror just the same. He thought he'd heard someone say, "Lady, your mouth is green!" Charlie had just turned on the inside lights to wake up the sleeping passengers before they pulled into town.

What he saw in the mirror was that the beautiful blonde lady with the white leather purse, the one in the fifth row center, had red lips with green edges! She looked like Mrs. Dracula! Her eyes were wide; she seemed surprised.

Charlie had to look at the road ahead. He couldn't wreck the bus just because of some lady wearing weird makeup. When he looked back, she was looking in her own little mirror. She looked as shocked as Charlie felt. Charlie had to look at the road again.

This time when Charlie looked at his inside mirror, her lips were pink—but still a little green around the edges. She was furiously scrubbing away at them with a little handkerchief which once might have been white. Charlie looked at the road again. They were nearing the bus station in this little town.

It was a few mintues before he could look again. When he did, the blonde lady was beautiful again. Her lips were red with no green edges. As the passengers were getting off at the bus station, the lady stopped to speak to Charlie.

"I looked pretty strange with eyeliner on my lips, didn't I?" she said. "When I did it, I thought I was using my lipliner."

The Answers

1. Touching up her lipliner. _____

_____

2. Mrs. Dracula. _____

3. Red, with green edges. _____

4. The bus driver. _____

5. White leather. _____

6. A little handkerchief. _____

7. ". . . once might have been white." _____

8. Pink. _____

Bonus Questions

A. What color was the lady's handkerchief after she scrubbed her lips with it?

_____

B. What would cause the lady to think that her eyeliner was lipliner?

_____

       What's the Question?

EXERCISE 19:

What's the Question?

Name _____

Date _____

One day that fall, as Brian was nearing his house, he glanced toward the backyard, and his eyes stopped on his old tree house. "I really am going to have to tear that old thing down," he thought. His mother had been after him for ages to get rid of the "eyesore," as she called it. "Oh, well," he said to himself, "when the season is over, I'll get around to it."

Then Christmas vacation was upon him before he realized it. Brian had been out of school for a few days when he remembered his promise to his mom about doing away with the tree house. He decided that he'd better get on the job right away, because there wasn't any snow on the tree. Besides, it wasn't very cold out.

He went out to the toolshed and gathered together the necessary equipment—a hammer, a wrecking bar,

and a rope—and headed out to the big oak tree in the backyard. He climbed the huge limbs to the center of the tree, and rested on one of the branches that itself was almost as big as an ordinary tree. Then he looked around at the neighborhood in which he had grown up. Things really had not changed that much, he thought.

"Well, I'll be . . . ," he said to himself. "Look at that old sled in back of Thompson's shed. Jack and I used to slide down the hill at Morrison's Pond on it! I remember one winter we thought the pond was frozen solid and Jack almost drowned when the sled went through the ice. He always called me his 'hero' after I pulled him out."

The Answers

1. Jack. _____

2. Fall and winter. _____

3. Oak. _____

4. In Brian's backyard. _____

5. In back of Thompson's shed. _____

6. A hammer, a wrecking bar, and a rope. _____

7. His hero. _____

8. Morrison's Pond. _____

Bonus Questions

A. What season did Brian want to end before he removed the tree house?

_____

B. How did Brian carry the hammer, wrecking bar, and rope when he climbed?

_____

What's the Question?

Name _____

Date _____

Brian watched and listened to the world below him. He could see children playing and chasing each other. From this height, their voices sounded muffled, but he could hear their laughter quite clearly. Laura's Irish setter was burying a bone beside their fence, and Ol' Dan was stalking something that was under the Morowskis' deck.

How peaceful this place was! He had almost forgotten. After all, he hadn't been in the tree house since he was ten or eleven. It had been a long time since Brian felt the way he did right now, and he wasn't ready to give up that feeling. He wondered how his mother would feel about a practically grown man wanting to keep an old tree house. Well, he would ask her, anyway. He climbed down.

"Brian," his mother said, "it would make me a little sad to see the tree house torn down, but it really does look bad."

"But Mom," Brian argued, "the leaves cover it in spring and summer, so it's only exposed for a few months."

"Sorry, Brian," she answered. "It has to go."

Brian went outside and climbed the big tree again. When he reached the tree house, he sat and let his mind drift back to the days of his childhood. Time stood still in this little place, and Brian was a ten-year-old boy again, stalking criminals and being the lookout for a pirate ship.

Night found him still reminiscing about the child that had sawed the boards and nailed the nails that created this wonderful place. Brian knew that he couldn't tear it down.

The Answers

1. A peaceful place. _____

2. He built the tree house. _____

3. It was burying a bone. _____

4. Stalking something. _____

5. Laughter. _____

6. Ten or eleven. _____

7. Brian's mother. _____

8. Muffled. _____

Bonus Questions

A. Why could Brian see below him through the branches of the big tree?

_____

B. What had Brian used when he had played in the tree house?

_____

What's the Question?

Name _____

Date _____

The old house frightened her. Marla didn't go there often. When she did, it was only out of respect for her lovely old great-grandmother. Gram had always lived in this house. When she and Marla's great-grandfather were married, they lived in the west wing. When Gram's parents passed away, the couple had become masters of the estate. They moved into the larger east wing and occupied the main area of the house.

Ever since she was tiny, Marla had feared the mansion. There was something strange about it. A weeping willow hung ominously over the east balcony.

A looming oak cast eerie shadows over the great house. Now Marla was sorry that on this night she had to go over and see about the old woman.

Marla found Gram lying in bed. She was pale. There was a strange look on her face. Her eyes were focused upward. Her arm looked as if it were reaching out for something. She was moving her lips. A very soft sound came from deep in her chest.

Marla tiptoed to the bed. She listened carefully. It was hard to understand what the old lady was saying. But it was no use. Gram's mumbling didn't make sense.

The Answers

1. The old mansion. _____

2. Marla. _____

3. Gram. _____

4. The west wing. _____

5. Deep in her chest. _____

6. Gram's mumbling. _____

7. A weeping willow. _____

8. Night. _____

Bonus Questions

A. Which is tallest—the oak, the willow, or the house?

_____

B. Where did Marla live?

_____

What's the Question?

Marla had reluctantly gone to see her great-grandmother. When she arrived at the mansion, she found Gram lying on the bed, staring upward and whispering incoherently. A slip of paper on the coverlet caught Marla's attention. She gingerly picked it up and began to read:

Clarissa,
  I shall come for you soon. Be ready at 9:00 P.M. on the anniversary of our vows. I love you and miss you.
                                          Charles

"Clarissa! That's Gram's name!" Marla thought. "And Gramps's name was Charles!" She was beginning to feel very frightened, and was on the verge of phoning her mother when the hall clock struck nine.

Marla stood stock still. Her eyes were on Gram, who lay with her hands across her chest. A radiant smile was on her lips. Something akin to a light rose from the bed. It slowly ascended to the ceiling and then was gone.

Marla stood in wonder and awe. Never had she felt such peace. The calm that pervaded the room was indescribable. Marla found herself smiling, too, just as the old woman had done a moment ago. She covered Gram with a quilt that lay at the foot of the bed. Then she turned around and walked out of the room and down the hall.

The Answers

1. Gram's name. _____

2. Incoherently. _____

3. Charles. _____

4. Nine. _____

5. A smile. _____

6. Peaceful. _____

7. A quilt. _____

8. Across her chest. _____

Bonus Questions

A. On what special day did this story happen?

_____

B. What is the unsolved question?

_____

What's the Question?

Name _____

Date _____

Harrison didn't think about it, but it was strange. The city's lights had all gone out at once. Probably some temporary problem at the power plant. It had been known to happen. It was usually during violent storms like this one. He lit all the candles he could find. Then he lit the camping lantern in the den.

Next he went into the bedroom to get his flashlight. He always kept it beside his bed. Then he decided that he ought to go next door to the Johnsons'. He thought he'd check on the mother and two small children. After all, they lived there alone. He knew they would be frightened. He thought that a friendly face would help calm them.

As he went out the front door, Harrison felt an unexplainable force about him. It wasn't just the lull in the storm. There was pressure in the air. He had the feeling that something strong was pressing against his body. It wasn't moving him as the wind would. Instead, it was pressing inward toward the center of his body. It seemed to compress his very being. He felt that he would suffocate if he didn't get inside before long.

As he made his way across the lawn, he was struggling for his very breath. At last he reached Mrs. Johnson's door. He knocked. She was nervous about letting someone in, so Harrison told her who was there. When she heard his voice, she swung open the door. She almost threw her arms around him!

Mrs. Johnson said that her children were fast asleep. Harrison gave her his flashlight and told her to stay inside. She promised him she would, and he promised to come back and check on her soon.

The Answers

1. The city's lights all went out. _____

2. He intended to calm them. _____

3. In the bedroom. _____

4. The mother of two small children. _____

5. Next door to Harrison. _____

6. Violent. _____

7. His flashlight. _____

8. To stay inside. _____

Bonus Questions

A. What would be a good title for this story?

_____

B. What do you think happened to Harrison as he went back to his own house?

_____

What's the Question?

Name _____

Date _____

There was a blackout in town. Harrison lit candles. Then he went next door to check on his neighbor and her children. On the way there he had an eerie feeling. It was a strange pressure against his body. Mrs. Johnson promised to stay inside as Harrision left.

As he was leaving the Johnsons', he felt the same eerie feeling, but the feeling was more pronounced now. Harrison hurried toward the shelter of his own roof.

Just as he approached his house, everything suddenly went black. All the candles and the lantern went out. He could not find the door. He panicked! He felt as if he could not breathe. He kept moving to the right and then to the left. All the time he was feeling for the doorknob. He knew it had to be somewhere in the door. But he could not find it. Darkness overcame him, and he knew no more.

Harrison awoke in a place filled with strange lights. He looked all around him, but he recognized nothing. Suddenly, two beings approached him. They carried tremendous knives in their hands. Harrison nearly passed out again! They were aliens! The aliens stood over him. They seemed to be talking about what a lovely Cratzoidanian dinner they were going to have. Then . . .

The Answers

1. Eerie. _____

2. It means to get inside his own house. _____

3. Cratzoidanian. _____

4. He was approaching his house. _____

5. He panicked and moved to the right and to the left. _____

6. Tremendous knives. _____

7. He passed out. _____

8. In a room filled with strange lights. _____

Bonus Questions

A. Could this story have really happened? Tell why you think as you do.

_____

B. What would you do if you were Harrison and the Cratzoidanians were ready to cut you up for dinner?

_____

EXERCISE 25:

What's the Question?

Name _____

Date _____

He was born in Dallas. By age seven he was playing a guitar, copying his older brother. By age thirteen he was appearing in Dallas clubs. Stevie Ray Vaughan kept on playing until he became one of the best-known guitarists in the world. In 1984, Stevie Ray and his band, Double Trouble, produced a platinum record, *Couldn't Stand the Weather.*

Stevie Ray's life had its share of ups and downs. In the early 1980's, his guitar jamming and his rocking Texas roadhouse blues style had won him two Grammy awards and taken him from Austin and San Antonio to London. His sound made one think of music legends B.B. King and Muddy Waters.

But during a performance in London in the mid-1980's, Stevie Ray Vaughan collapsed. He had become a drug addict. For about two weeks he had been unable to get the drugs he needed. Because he couldn't get

drugs, he drank constantly. He was drunk most of the time for two weeks before he collapsed.

Collapsing on tour probably saved his life, because it made Stevie Ray realize that he had to get off drugs and alcohol. And he did. He took drug treatments and licked both drugs and alcohol. And when he did, his music got better and better.

Then one Saturday night, late in August of 1990, he gave a concert in Wisconsin. After the concert, Stevie Ray got in a helicopter. It was to take him to Chicago, but it never arrived. At 7:00 the next morning, its wreckage was found. The great guitarist was dead. On the following Monday night, hundreds of fans held candlelight vigils in Austin and San Antonio. Many wore T-shirts from his concerts. Some also wore copies of his wide-brimmed Texas hat.

The Answers

1. Rocking Texas roadhouse blues. _____

2. In a helicopter crash. _____

3. In late August, 1990. _____

4. Dallas, Texas. _____

5. He couldn't get drugs. _____

6. The music of B.B. King and Muddy Waters. _____

7. *Couldn't Stand the Weather.* _____

8. Stevie Ray collapsed. _____

Bonus Questions

A. Why did fans hold a candlelight vigil and dress up in clothes that reminded them of Stevie Ray Vaughan?

_____

B. If Stevie Ray Vaughan had continued to drink and take drugs, would he still be alive today? Would he be a big star? Why or why not?

_____

© 1991 J. Weston Walch, Publisher   25   *What's the Question?*

What's the Question?

Stephanie and Corey were best friends. They had known each other since kindergarten. Stephanie remembered the first day of school. Corey had knocked her down trying to get to the slide first. She didn't like him then. But through the years they had grown together. Now neither had a better friend in the world.

It was so easy for Stephanie to talk to Corey. They shared their dreams and their disappointments. They laughed together and cried together. While they were in middle school, their friend Rob had died in an automobile accident. Stephanie and Corey went to the funeral together. Then they spent that whole afternoon just walking along the riverbank, talking about Rob. Corey was a sweet and caring young man, and Stephanie loved being with him. She loved him more than she could say.

It wasn't at all surprising that Corey asked Stephanie to marry him. She said yes, of course. Then they set the date of the wedding for late fall. The wedding was lovely. The red, orange, and yellow leaves in her backyard decorated the beautiful ceremony. The two were extremely happy. Each was certain that the love that had grown with their close friendship was sure to last a lifetime.

The Answers

1. Late fall. _____

2. Rob. _____

3. Dreams and disappointments. _____

4. In Stephanie's backyard. _____

5. To the slide. _____

6. Corey. _____

7. A lifetime. _____

8. Kindergarten. _____

Bonus Questions

A. Does anything about the way this is written suggest that the marriage may not last? If so, what is it?

_____

B. Which character is best developed by the author? What clues is the reader given to that character's personality?

_____

What's the Question?

Name _____

Date _____

In 1964, about 120 mother loggerheads nested on Cumberland Island. In 1989, there were only 24. Nothing seems to be able to save the giant sea turtles from extinction.

The mother turtles come in out of the ocean for only a little over an hour. Sometime during the night they skid up the beach, using their flippers, and dig a foot-deep hole in the warm sand. Then they lay eggs at the rate of one every 10 seconds or so until there are over 100 in the hollow of the sand. Using their back flippers, the mothers cover the eggs with sand and then skid back to the water. They may come back to lay eggs four or five times during the summer. Then they will not usually return for at least three more years.

Many of the eggs, which are shaped like Ping-Pong balls, are eaten by wild pigs and raccoons that live along the coast. When the baby turtles hatch and try to get their little silver-dollar shapes into the sea, gulls and other shore birds feast on their tender bodies.

However, animal predators are not the main reason for the loss of the great turtles. Boats trawling for shrimp and fish catch the big turtles in their nets. Since turtles breathe air, the nets drown them by holding them under water. Friends of the great sea turtles hope that soon all shrimp-fishing boats will have turtle-exclusion devices that will release turtles from their nets without drowning them. Only if the fishing boats start using these devices will the turtles be saved.

The Answers

1. Fishing trawlers' nets. _____

2. Turtle-exclusion devices. _____

3. 120. _____

4. Three. _____

5. Four or five times. _____

6. One foot. _____

7. One every 10 seconds. _____

8. 24. _____

Bonus Questions

A. How many Cumberland Island mother turtles may have been lost from the group that should have returned in 1989?

_____

B. How do you think the shrimp fishermen feel about using turtle-exclusion devices on their nets?

_____

What's the Question?

Name _____

Date _____

For a shy sixteen-year-old girl, Molly was really getting into the spotlight lately! However, it was not exactly the kind of attention anyone, let alone someone like Molly, would welcome. It seemed that every time she turned around these days, something embarrassing was happening to her.

For starters, on her very first day at Jefferson High School, Molly got out of her mother's car and shut the door on her skirt. Her mom drove off, not knowing that Molly was still attached to the car, and almost dragged Molly through the school parking lot. Molly ran alongside the car, screaming and banging on the door handle, and finally got her mom's attention. Kids all around were laughing and pointing at the sight.

Molly wished the ground would open up and swallow her right then and there.

As if that were not enough, two days later Molly was late to school and ran into Spanish class just under the wire. She slid into a seat and began listening to the lecture, which should have been an overview of Spanish history, when it began to dawn on her that the teacher was not talking about Spain at all; the lesson was on Greek mythology. Molly was in the wrong room! She didn't want to be reported absent by her Spanish teacher, so she quickly got up and tiptoed to the door. As she turned the knob, she heard several students snicker and others whisper, and she wished she were somewhere else, like on Mars or Venus.

The Answers

1. Jefferson High School. _____

2. In her mother's car. _____

3. Molly's skirt. _____

4. Spanish. _____

5. Greek mythology. _____

6. Report her absent. _____

7. Tiptoed to the door. _____

8. Snicker and whisper. _____

Bonus Questions

A. In what grade was Molly?

_____

B. Do you think things will get better for Molly, or will she drop out of school?

_____

What's the Question?

Name _____

Date _____

When Molly entered a new school, things started out all wrong. When her mother dropped her off the first morning in the school parking lot, she got her skirt caught in the car door and put on a show for all to see. Then she plopped down in a seat in the wrong classroom and had to run out in front of everyone. Molly thought that nothing more humiliating could possibly happen. But those embarrassing moments were nothing compared to what happened on the day of the Student Council meeting.

Molly had been so pleased that her classmates had elected her to serve on the council; rarely had a newcomer at school been elected to the student government, she had been told. And on the morning of the first meeting, Molly was glowing. She had worn her best outfit and had spent more than two hours before school grooming herself and making sure that every hair was in place and that all of her makeup was perfect.

Molly arrived on time and looking lovely. Everything was going in her favor. Josh Desmond, the most gorgeous guy Molly had ever seen in her entire life, was presiding. He introduced Molly and asked her to come to the mike and say a few words about herself.

Molly was so nervous, she thought she would die. Her mouth felt as if she had cotton in it. The more she talked, the worse it became. All of a sudden, her tongue stuck to her retainer, which flew out of her mouth and arched over the podium. Josh Desmond made a dive for it and caught it, amid laughter and cheers from all of the other council members. Molly was mortified! As she reached out to retrieve the retainer, down she went! The kids went wild! Molly got up and ran out, vowing that she would never set foot in Jefferson High School again.

The Answers

1. Mike. _____

2. Jefferson High School. _____

3. Josh Desmond. _____

4. The Student Council. _____

5. Rarely. _____

6. A gorgeous guy. _____

7. Her tongue stuck to it. _____

8. Glowing. _____

Bonus Questions

A. What do these words mean: "Put on a show for all to see"?

_____

B. Why did Molly's mouth feel as if there was cotton in it? How can we know Molly was afraid?

_____

What's the Question?

Name _____

Date _____

The price of baseball cards is going up! A Honus Wagner baseball card was recently sold for $100,000. A Mickey Mantle rookie card in mint condition is worth about $5,000 or more. A complete set put out by Topps Bubble Gum in 1957 is now worth about $6,000.

The first baseball cards were printed in the early 1900's. Tobacco companies gave out the cards with packages of their products. Eventually, the makers of bubble gum started producing the cards, and from 1955 until 1980 one manufacturer, Topps, had a monopoly on baseball cards.

Since 1980, four other companies have begun making baseball cards: Donruss, Score, Fleer, and Upper Deck. However, these companies are not allowed to distribute their cards with bubble gum. Topps is still the only company allowed to do that, but some dealers wish they would stop. The bubble gum often stains the cards.

During the 1980's, cards for other sports began to be printed. Now you can get hockey cards, basketball cards, and football cards.

The early cards cost 5 cents when purchased with sheets of bubble gum that were the same size as the cards. Now you can still buy the cards in packs of 16, but they'll cost you between 50 cents and 2 dollars. Many buyers simply buy a complete set that contains one of each card produced by the manufacturer in that year. A set costs $24 or more. Once the manufacturer has printed its set for a particular year, it never revises it and it never prints any more. So the buyers plan to hold the cards until their value goes up before selling them. They read the *Beckett Monthly* magazine in order to keep up on what cards are worth how much. Remember, a complete 1957 Topps set is worth at least $6,000.

The Answers

1. Topps. _____

2. Five cents. _____

3. $24 or more. _____

4. Tobacco companies. _____

5. Honus Wagner. _____

6. $5,000. _____

7. A monopoly. _____

8. In mint condition. _____

Bonus Questions

A. Why did companies start making baseball cards?

_____

B. How much will older baseball cards cost you now?

_____

What's the Question?

Name _____

Date _____

Crystal is Jackie Jennings' pet. Crystal has black eyes and pure white fur. She fits into Jackie's purse and she doesn't make a sound there. When she's out of the purse, she gives Jackie little kisses.

Crystal is a rat. Jackie is vice president of the American Fancy Rat and Mouse Association. The association has 150 members in southern California. They get together to show off their pet rats and mice. These fancy pets come in all sorts of colors. Some are lilac and amber.

The president of the association is Leona Pasley. Leona says that the first people to make pets of rats and mice were the English. They started back in the 1700's. However, rats are still not very well-liked pets, even though they're cheap. A really fine rat costs only about $10.

The association prints a newsletter twice a month. It has letters and poems from all over. It even has a crossword puzzle. The newsletter is called *Rat and Mouse Tales.*

The Answers

1. Little kisses. _____

2. 150. _____

3. The English. _____

4. $10. _____

5. *Rat and Mouse Tales.* _____

6. Twice a month. _____

7. Jackie Jennings. _____

8. Crystal. _____

Bonus Questions

A. Would you like to have a mouse or rat for a pet? Why or why not?

_____

B. Why has Jackie trained Crystal not to make any noise when the rat is in Jackie's purse?

_____

EXERCISE 32:

What's the Question?

Name _____

Date _____

Ulysses is aimed at the sun. It will take five years to get there. The sun is 93 million miles away, but *Ulysses* is moving at thousands of miles an hour.

Ulysses was fired from the NASA shuttle *Discovery*. Firing off the satellite was one of the crew's jobs. *Discovery* was in orbit around the earth at the time.

The astronauts had a nearly perfect mission. They blasted off from Cape Canaveral and made it into

Earth's orbit. They did everything they were supposed to do. There had been no problems.

Then, on the Tuesday before *Discovery* returned, a heater unit failed. Luckily, Houston Mission Control was able to start a backup heater. It warmed the power unit so that *Discovery* could land at Edwards Air Force Base. *Discovery* completed its mission on October 9, 1990. The weather was good and the shuttle's landing was perfect. It landed at 6:57 A.M.

The Answers

1. Cape Canaveral. _____

2. *Ulysses.* _____

3. Five years. _____

4. 93 million miles. _____

5. Thousands of miles per hour. _____

6. *Discovery.* _____

7. Edwards Air Force Base. _____

8. 6:57 A.M., October 9, 1990. _____

Bonus Questions

A. Why was *Ulysses* fired from the *Discovery* instead of being fired from Earth?

_____

B. How fast will *Ulysses* travel on its voyage to the sun?

_____

32 *What's the Question?*

What's the Question?

It happened on October 15, 1987, at the International Hot Rod Association's Chief Auto Parts Nationals. Richard Holcombe became the third man to break five seconds for the quarter mile. Only two others had done it previously: Eddie Hill of Wichita Falls, Texas, and Gene Snow of Fort Worth.

But Holcombe's 4.99-second run was even more remarkable than the two earlier runs. The reason was that his Top Fuel Dragster did it with an old spare engine that hadn't even had its clutch set properly.

Holcombe's first run that day had gone well. He thought he would have a good day, but he soon changed his mind. When Holcombe ran his second qualifying pass, his clutch exploded and broke the bell housing. The engine was too badly damaged to repair.

But Holcombe's team put in the old spare engine that they thought was worn out. They guessed at the clutch setting, and Holcombe climbed in and went for it. Just 4.99 seconds later, the man and his car were in drag racing's record books. That old wornout engine had given Holcombe his fastest speed ever: 277.89 miles per hour.

The Answers

1. The third man to break the five-second barrier. _____

2. Holcombe's time for the run. _____

3. The clutch on the spare engine. _____

4. Wichita Falls, Texas. _____

5. Gene Snow. _____

6. The Chief Auto Parts Nationals. _____

7. The International Hot Rod Association. _____

8. Holcombe's fastest speed ever. _____

Bonus Questions

A. Why did Holcombe's team install the old spare engine?

_____

B. What do you think they did with the engine after Holcombe won with it?

_____

What's the Question?

Name _____

Date _____

Are you depressed? Have you had the blues for several days? Are you always down in the mouth? Are you a hopeless case? If you feel down all the time, you're not alone. You are one of perhaps 20 million Americans who suffer from depression. Nearly 10 percent of all American men have this illness at some time in their lives, as do more than 20 percent of American women.

Depression is true mental anguish. It is constant grief without a clear cause, and although it's treatable, it can be deadly if left untreated. Yet only a third of the people who have it seek help, and those who haven't had it can't understand it at all.

Harold Eist, a psychiatrist from Bethesda, Maryland, says that its severest form, clinical depression, is deadly. "Clinically depressed patients are filled with despair and self-hatred," he says. "Finally, their pain is so great that the only way out they can see is to destroy themselves."

Yet many famous people have somehow endured it. Abraham Lincoln had it and Winston Churchill called it "the black dog on my back." Of course, Lincoln and Churchill may have had a milder form of depression called dysthymia.

People with depression need to know that help is available. Antidepressant drugs can help many sufferers. Talk therapy, which is cheaper than traditional psychoanalysis, is beginning to help many others. And there is a last resort, shock therapy, in which the victim's brain is given convulsions by exposing it to a mild electric current. It seems like a terrible thing to endure, but sufferers from true depression will tell you that it's a price worth paying.

The Answers

1. True mental anguish. _____

2. Nearly 10 percent. _____

3. More than 20 percent. _____

4. Antidepressant drugs, talk therapy, psychoanalysis, shock therapy. _____

5. A psychiatrist from Bethesda, Maryland. _____

6. Famous people who suffered from depression. _____

7. 20 million. _____

8. Dysthymia. _____

Bonus Questions

A. What might be common symptoms of severe clinical depression?

_____

B. If you were depressed, would you want shock therapy?

_____

What's the Question?

Name _____

Date _____

At one time, most of the people who entered flight school were military veterans who had government financial assistance for their schooling. Now, however, many flight students are young people hoping to make flying a career.

Clint Rodgers, the chief pilot and manager of a big flight school, says that there are good opportunities for young people to make a living by flying. "It's a long road and the pay's not great at first," he said. "But you can get started in a flight school. Then you get experience and you might get a job on a regional airline."

If you want to be a pilot, you must first fly with an instructor. To get an instructor, you'll probably need to contact a flight school. Most beginners solo after about 15 hours in the air. But they must also get 35 hours of ground school instruction and they must fly at least 20 more hours before they can apply for a private pilot's license. Finally, each student must perform a check-ride with an examiner on board and must pass a written test.

Of course, all of that costs money—the plane rental, the cost of the instructor's time, and the fuel. The total cost is usually between $2,500 and $4,000. Most people complete the course in a few months' time, but some spread it out over years. But that's not all. To get "instrument-rated" or "multi-engine rated," one must meet many more requirements.

The Answers

1. Not great at first. _____

2. Fly with an instructor. _____

3. Chief pilot and manager of a big flight school. _____

4. Young people. _____

5. Between $2,500 and $4,000. _____

6. Check-ride. _____

7. 35 hours. _____

8. A regional airline. _____

Bonus Questions

A. What is the next step up after a pilot gets experience with a regional airline?

_____

B. How many total hours of flying and schooling are required before one can apply for a private pilot's license?

_____

What's the Question?

Name _____

Date _____

It was a sad time at Jefferson County High School. Chad Montgomery had been killed in an automobile accident. Everyone said that it was Frank Hoffman's fault. No one really knew, though. Frank was still in the hospital in Intensive Care. The doctors weren't even sure that he would live.

The football team held a memorial service for Chad. He had been their first-string quarterback, and he surely would be missed. He was not only a great player but also a really wonderful human being. Everybody liked Chad. It just didn't seem possible that he was dead.

The day before the accident, Chad had been kidding around with some of the other players. He told

them that he had made a decision. He said he'd announce it at the next practice. Everybody figured it had something to do with Melanie. He had been dating her for two years. Maybe he was going to give her a ring. The junior-senior prom was coming up next week, and it would be the perfect place for something like that.

But now they would never know. Melanie wondered about it at the funeral. What was on his mind? Was he really going to propose to her? She knew she'd spend the rest of her life wondering. Her eyes filled with tears.

The Answers

1. Frank Hoffman. _____

2. An automobile accident. _____

3. Chad Montgomery. _____

4. Jefferson County High School. _____

5. Two years. _____

6. Quarterback. _____

7. Melanie. _____

8. The junior-senior prom. _____

Bonus Questions

A. Why do you suppose people were blaming Frank Hoffman? What kind of person do you think Frank might have been? Is it right for people to blame the person who lived? Why?

_____

B. Do you think Melanie loved Chad? What would she have said if he'd asked her to marry him?

_____

EXERCISE 37:

What's the Question?

Name _____

Date _____

Cats don't really have nine lives, but they sometimes seem to escape death when there is no hope. Boogs was a six-year-old Wisconsin cat that nipped the animal control officer who had come to pick him up. It seems that Boogs, a big grey-and-white bully, had growled at his neighbors and eaten their cat's food. The Madison City Health Department had decided to put Boogs to death, and for fifteen months he lived in a cage on "Death Row" at the Dane County Animal Shelter.

But Boogs's owners went to court and got him off. A state judge ruled that he could go free—almost. His owners would have to keep him inside the house, or he would have to be on a leash and muzzled, or he would have to be caged. But at least Boogs is still alive—and he has eight lives yet to go!

A cat in Grafton, Virginia, came even closer to dying than Boogs did. This cat, Shadow, was a $300 blue-point Himalayan that apparently went more than a month with no food or water. Shadow disappeared in July 1990 and was found 37 days later in a vending machine, a shadow of her plump former self. Her owner, Daressa Hooper, said that Shadow had lost three pounds but that she seemed to be all right. "She's up to her old loving tricks," Ms. Hooper said.

The Answers

1. Nine lives. _____
2. Daressa Hooper. _____
3. Madison, Wisconsin. _____
4. A six-year-old cat. _____
5. 37 days. _____
6. Grey and white. _____
7. A state judge. _____
8. Grafton, Virginia. _____

Bonus Questions

A. On all of those 37 days when she was missing, was Shadow inside the machine?

_____

B. How did Shadow survive without water?

_____

What's the Question?

Name _____

Date _____

They left England in April 1587 in five little ships. There were 115 of them, including two pregnant women. They dared to cross the Atlantic to settle a colony in the New World. Their leader was John White, an artist friend of Sir Walter Raleigh. As the appointed governor of the new colony, White was responsible for its well-being. His eighteen-year-old daughter, Elenor Dare, was one of the two pregnant women among the settlers. She was the wife of Ananias Dare, one of White's assistants.

The commander of the fleet of ships was in a hurry. He left a small amount of food and supplies and hurried off, with four of the five ships. The settlers soon built a village of crude log houses on Roanoke Island, which is now part of the state of Virginia. And in this settlement White's daughter, Elenor, gave birth to the first English child born in America, Virginia Dare.

But White could not stay long. The settlement's supplies and food dwindled rapidly. In August of 1587, he and his son-in-law went back to England for more. Unfortunately, in 1587 and 1588 England needed all of its ships to fight the Spanish Armada. White and Dare could not go back to Roanoke Island.

Dusk was settling when John White stepped ashore on Roanoke Island three years after he had left. There were footprints on the ground and the remains of a log fire. The letters C-R-O were carved on a tree and the word *CROATOAN* was carved on a post driven into the ground. At first this gave them some hope, because Croatoan was the settlers' name for what is now called Hatteras Island. However, on Croatoan there was no sign of the colonists. And now, 400 years later, we still can only guess at the fate of those settlers. Modern Americans call their settlement "The Lost Colony."

The Answers

1. Roanoke Island. _____

2. Two. _____

3. John White. _____

4. John White's daughter, a pregnant woman. _____

5. 1587. _____

6. The first English child born in America. _____

7. To fight the Spanish Armada. _____

8. Hatteras Island. _____

Bonus Questions

A. What do you think happened to the settlers of the Lost Colony? Why?

_____

B. Should John White have taken the colonists back to England when their supplies ran low?

_____

       What's the Question?

What's the Question?

Name _____

Date _____

Snakes are the most peculiar creatures in nature. They are found all over the world, except at the North and South Poles and on some ocean islands. Three types of snakes exist: poisonous, nonpoisonous, and constrictive. Poisonous snakes have fangs through which they inject venom into their prey or enemies, thereby killing them. Constrictors kill their prey or enemies by squeezing them to death. Nonpoisonous snakes must outwit their prey or enemies. These snakes are harmless to humans, and can even be of great benefit.

Snakes have no legs; however, some families, such as pythons and boas, have the remains of hind legs. These tiny legs are embedded in their bodies, and only spurs show outside. The absence of legs does not hinder the snake in moving around, though. Its muscles contract, allowing the scales on its underside to push against irregularities in the ground and propel itself forward.

The snake devours its prey by swallowing it whole. Some snakes swallow their prey alive; others kill by means of poison or constriction, and then swallow their prey. The snake's jaws are connected by elastic ligaments. This allows the snake to open its jaws wide in order to devour prey much bigger than itself. As the prey is swallowed, digestive enzymes dissolve it so that it can be absorbed into the snake's bloodstream.

The Answers

1. Poisonous, nonpoisonous, constrictive. _____
_____

2. North Pole, South Pole, some ocean islands. _____
_____

3. Venom. _____

4. Squeezes it. _____

5. Embedded in their bodies. _____

6. Elastic ligaments. _____

7. Its jaws open wide. _____

8. Digestive enzymes. _____

Bonus Questions

A. What are some locations where one would not expect to find snakes?

_____

B. Do you think snakes would have difficulty moving on very smooth surfaces? Why or why not?

_____

What's the Question?

Around the world, thousands of teenage soldiers have been forced to fight. The United Nations estimated that 200,000 children under the age of fifteen were fighting in the forty or more wars going on from Afghanistan to Peru in 1990.

One place in which very young soldiers have fought is El Salvador. The president of El Salvador, Alfredo Cristiani, said in July 1990 that his country's army had traditionally filled its ranks by finding young men on the street. "I don't really think that that is the best way to recruit," he went on. "For the past ten years, it has been the custom. I guess it started with the war and it just kept on going. No one enters our army voluntarily—and the young men ignore their draft notices."

In Honduras, President Rafael Callejas claimed that his army didn't draft people under eighteen. But then hundreds of high school students picketed him. They said that they knew his army had grabbed at least thirty students who had been waiting at bus stops.

In Guatemala, a story is told about a telegram sent to the president of the country by one of the generals. "I'm sending you 500 volunteers," it said. "Please send back the ropes."

But in Nicaragua, teenagers are smiling. In 1990, the new president, Violeta Chamarro, ended the draft. "We used to stay inside all the time," said one of them. "We didn't want to die for nothing. Now we can go wherever we want. We aren't afraid anymore."

The Answers

1. Thousands of teenagers. _____

2. Ten years. _____

3. Violeta Chamarro. _____

4. Draft notices. _____

5. They picketed their president. _____

6. At bus stops. _____

7. The draft ended. _____

8. 200,000. _____

Bonus Questions

A. According to the joke, how would the president of Guatemala get a lot of ropes?

_____

B. Is it wrong for teenagers to fight in wars if they really do volunteer to fight?

_____

What's the Question?

Name _____

Date _____

It stands for Light Amplified Stimulated Emission of Radiation. You've heard it called *LASER*. It's a very powerful beam of light that can burn holes in steel beams in less than a second. Laser beams are used to cut metals, to print letters and words on paper, to operate on people's eyes, to carry telephone messages, to read laser disks, and to put on light shows for everyone to enjoy—like fireworks displays. Because laser beams travel long distances without spreading out, they don't get weaker as they shoot through space. Because of this feature, they may well become our most important form of telecommunication in the space age.

Ordinary light rays travel in all directions, spreading out as they travel. They have many different wavelengths so that their light is many-colored and no one color is visible to our eyes.

A laser beam is started in a laser gun by a weak flash of light of just one wavelength. The rays in a laser beam all move in exactly the same direction, and all the rays in that beam have the same wavelength as the flash of light that started it. Therefore, the light beam is made of rays that are all the same color. The light waves of the rays in the beam are all in step. When they are in step, the crest of each ray is lined up with the crests of all the other rays. Light rays that are in step are very powerful. That's why laser beams can do what they do.

The Answers

1. Light Amplified Stimulated Emission of Radiation. _____

2. The same as the flash of light that started it. _____

3. Ordinary light rays. _____

4. Rays in a laser beam. _____

5. They have the same wavelength. _____

6. Each crest is lined up with the crests of the other rays. _____

7. Different wavelengths. _____

8. Just one. _____

Bonus Questions

A. What happens to ordinary light rays as they spread out traveling through space?

_____

B. Why does laser-printed paper smell as though it has been burned?

_____

     What's the Question?

What's the Question?

Members of the National Guard are citizen soldiers who play an important role in plans for the defense of the United States. In 1978, Secretary of Defense Melvin Laird made the Guard part of his "Total Force" plan. Because he did so, Guard members are no longer backups to the regular Army and the reserves. Now National Guard members must have the same training as regular soldiers. They must go to the same schools and be able to use the same weapons and equipment as Army regulars.

One general said, "The Guard used to train with wheelbarrows and broomsticks. Members only trained 39 days a year, one weekend a month, and 15 days in summer camp. Now members must spend an average of 67 days in training during each year. A commander probably has to spend 100 days per year. It's hard to do that and work five days every week at a job. It's even harder to do it, hold a job, and be a good citizen in other ways—to raise kids, to be a community volunteer, to vote, to support the schools, or to join community organizations."

The National Guard is often the first group called upon when disaster strikes. When Hurricane Hugo battered South Carolina, the governor immediately called up 7,200 Guard members who had to leave their jobs and families until they were no longer needed to help victims of the disaster.

Guard members join for many reasons. Some need the extra pay; it's a high-paying part-time job. Others get to travel all over the world at government expense. Others join the Guard so they can go to college with nearly all expenses paid. And nearly all Guard members like doing something for their country.

The Answers

1. Wheelbarrows and broomsticks. _____

2. Melvin Laird. _____

3. 39. _____

4. 67. _____

5. 100. _____

6. South Carolina. _____

7. The governor of South Carolina. _____

8. Total Force. _____

Bonus Questions

A. What are some names people call members of the National Guard?

_____

B. Why might Guard members need to travel to many places?

_____

What's the Question?

Name _____

Date _____

They had to be flying daredevils; they fought the Japanese in the skies of South China and Burma when they were usually outnumbered ten to one. They were the American Volunteer Group, but Americans remember them as "The Flying Tigers." They had a toothy snarl painted on the nose of each of their P-40 Warhawk fighter planes.

Some of the more famous of the pilots were Tex Hill, Ed Rector, and Pappy Boyington. Their squadrons had names like the "Adams and Eves," "The Panda Bears," and "Hell's Angels." The commander of the group was Claire Lee Chennault, a retired Army captain who served as a consultant to the Chinese Air Force and who was a colonel in the Chinese Air Force.

Jim Howard was in the second squadron, "The Panda Bears." After fighting in China and Burma, he was sent to fight in Europe. He won the Congressional Medal of Honor, America's highest award, for aerial combat over Germany.

Parker Dupuoy was in the third squadron, "Hell's Angels." On Christmas Day, 1941, a Japanese Zero crashed into his P-40 and sheared four feet off his right wing. Dupuoy stayed with his P-40 and somehow flew it back to his base.

In July 1942, the U.S. Air Force assumed control of the air war in Asia. That's when Chennault and his Flying Tigers became part of the American Air Force.

The Answers

1. "The Panda Bears." _____

2. Claire Lee Chennault. _____

3. "Hell's Angels." _____

4. Over Germany. _____

5. America's highest award. _____

6. Aerial combat. _____

7. A toothy snarl. _____

8. China and Burma. _____

Bonus Questions

A. What squadron was called the "Adams and Eves"?

_____

B. Why did Americans fight for China before America entered the war against Japan?

_____

What's the Question?

Name _____

Date _____

Many different species of trees flourish on our planet and provide us with a majesty and beauty unparalleled by any other form of plant life. However, their beauty is only one reason why trees are such splended creations; they also hold a major position in the ecological balance of our earth.

Trees are masterpieces of nature. In the spring-time, in northern climates, their lovely, sweet-smelling blossoms give us assurance that life goes on; they give us a welcome break from the harsh and barren winter. Their green umbrellas provide us with coolness and shade in the summer months. In the fall, their foliage dazzles us with colors so vibrant that we can hardly imagine them. Only in the winter months do they sleep,

and even then they cast lovely dark images on the stark white snow; the evergreens provide the only color the winter knows.

Aside from their obvious beauty, their importance in our ecological system cannot be overstated. Trees take in noxious carbon dioxide that we breathe out and miraculously transform it into oxygen that helps to sustain all life. By controlling the amount of carbon dioxide in the air, trees provide us with a natural thermostat that helps to regulate the earth's temperature. The tropical rain forests actually create rain, cooling our planet and replenishing the earth with moisture that is constantly being evaporated from it.

The Answers

1. Carbon dioxide. _____

2. Provide a thermostat that helps to regulate it. _____

3. The rain forests. _____

4. Green umbrellas. _____

5. Masterpieces of nature. _____

6. On the snow. _____

7. Noxious. _____

8. Evergreens. _____

Bonus Questions

A. What does it mean to *replenish?*

_____

B. Why are scientists concerned about our planet's rain forests?

_____

What's the Question?

Name _____

Date _____

Are you interested in games? In some colleges students are learning to play *toli*, an ancient Indian game something like lacrosse. There are two versions; a Choctaw version, which is not violent, and a Cherokee version, which is. Modern players usually play the Choctaw version, and although Choctaw tradition excludes females, some of today's players are women. In the Cherokee version, players can be tackled at any time, even when they don't have the ball. Furthermore, Cherokee players often use their long sticks like clubs. In the Choctaw game, players are not supposed to club each other or tackle players who are not carrying the ball.

The game of toli is played outdoors. Players each carry two long, slender hickory sticks with the tips tied in loops that hold small baskets. The baskets can hold the tiny leather ball with which the game is played. They can also be used to throw or catch the little ball.

Two teams of 25 players each try to make the ball hit a 12-foot-high goal pole. When the ball hits or touches the pole, the team of the player who is holding it, or who threw it, scores.

You can't buy toli sticks in sporting-goods stores. If you want to play, you'll have to find a place where people have begun to enjoy this ancient game. You might find it being played on an Indian reservation. Some Navajo Indians in Arizona play. You might also find students playing toli at a college near you.

The Answers

1. The Cherokee version. _____

2. Little baskets on the ends of their sticks. _____

3. Toli. _____

4. By touching or hitting the goal pole with the ball. _____

5. A team. _____

6. The Choctaw version. _____

7. Two. _____

8. The goal pole. _____

Bonus Questions

A. How are jai alai and lacrosse like toli and how are they different?

_____

B. Should people be encouraged to play the Cherokee version of toli? Why or why not?

_____

     What's the Question?

What's the Question?

Name _____

Date _____

Forecasting the weather in early America was not an easy job. Pioneers didn't have the sophisticated equipment to predict rain or hot, dry weather. However, their livelihood often depended on guessing what the weather would be. Their crops could be lost and their farm animals could freeze to death if they guessed wrong.

Because the weather was so very important to them, the early settlers were always thinking up ways to predict it. Weather folklore became part of the education of early Americans and is still relied upon by many of us today.

One of the things pioneers noticed was that fur on animals was thicker at some times than at others. They observed that when the animals' fur was extremely thick, the winter was unusually harsh. Conversely, when the fur was not so thick, the winter was milder.

So they began to predict what kind of winter to expect by carefully observing the fur of animals.

Pioneers used their olfactory senses to predict rain. A person might sniff the air and determine whether or not it "smelled like rain." They depended on their sense of hearing to alert them to a change in temperature; a screech owl or a cricket would sound different when the temperature began to rise.

Some of the observations of the pioneers had foundations in science and proved to be very reliable. One such observation is "Red sky in the morning, sailors take warning!" Other observations have turned out to be nothing more than superstitions. But even in our day of technological sophistication, many people trust our weather folklore more than they trust the forecasting of the modern-day meteorologist.

The Answers

1. Sophisticated equipment. _____

2. The animals' fur was thick. _____

3. A reliable prediction. _____

4. They guessed wrong. _____

5. Weather folklore. _____

6. Pioneers and settlers. _____

7. Olfactory sense. _____

8. The meteorologist. _____

Bonus Questions

A. Was the weather more important to people in the past than it is to us today?

_____

B. What would be a good title for this passage?

_____

What's the Question?

Name _____

Date _____

The C.S.S. *Alabama*, a Confederate battleship, was branded as a "pirate ship" by Abraham Lincoln. It was a steam-and-sail ship which prowled international waters, terrorizing Union merchant ships. Before its watery death, it traveled 75,000 miles, captured 442 vessels, destroyed 55 of them, and seized more than 5 million dollars in supplies.

The feared battleship was commanded by Captain Raphael Semmes. He was nicknamed "Old Beeswax" because of his tremendous waxed moustache. Captain Semmes was from Mobile, Alabama. He was the only crew member from Alabama. A few members of the crew were Georgians, but most were from England, where the ship was built. Its designer was James Dunwoody Bulloch of Roswell, Georgia, who supervised its construction in England.

The vessel was sunk in a duel five miles off the coast of Cherbourg, France, more than 100 years ago, in 1864. It had been the Civil War's most notorious battleship.

In 1990, Gordon P. Watts, an underwater archaeologist, was the first American to see the remains of this once well-known vessel. He said that time had taken its toll. He estimated that only a third of the ship could be exhumed from its watery grave.

The Answers

1. The C.S.S. *Alabama*. _____

2. Abraham Lincoln. _____

3. James Dunwoody Bulloch. _____

4. Raphael Semmes. _____

5. Mobile, Alabama. _____

6. England. _____

7. Union merchant ships. _____

8. Its "watery death." _____

Bonus Questions

A. Where did Gordon Watts first see the C.S.S. *Alabama*?

_____

B. What does *C.S.S.* stand for?

_____

What's the Question?

The sunken ruin of the C.S.S. *Alabama* was first discovered in French waters. It was thought that France would keep the battleship. However, the French government gave it to the United States. Now there is an argument. People can't agree on where it should go.

Alabamans think that the ship should be given to them. It was named after their state. Raphael Semmes, the ship's captain, was a native of Alabama. Georgians argue that it was designed by a Georgian. They add that many of the crew members were from Georgia. Also, Columbus, Georgia, is the home of the Confederate Naval Museum. This museum is the only one in the world exclusively devoted to the Confederate Navy. Georgians say it is the best place for the ship.

However, the ship was built in England. The majority of the crew members were from that country. Therefore, the British claim that the ship should come to them. Finally, East Carolina University claims the ship. Their Dr. Watts, an archaeology professor, was the first American to view the remains. Other states and other societies also hope that they will get it. Where will the C.S.S. *Alabama* spend the rest of its days? That is a question that as yet has no answer.

The Answers

1. The United States. _____

2. Columbus, Georgia. _____

3. A confederate battleship. _____

4. France's. _____

5. England. _____

6. An archaeologist from East Carolina University. _____

7. The only museum in the world devoted exclusively to the Confederate Navy. _____

    _____

8. Captain Semmes. _____

Bonus Questions

A. What is so wonderful about the C.S.S. *Alabama* that makes so many groups want it? Will having it somehow improve their lot? Explain.

    _____

B. Which group do you think should get the remains? Why?

    _____

     What's the Question?

What's the Question?

Born in Charleston, Massachusetts, in 1791, Samuel F.B. Morse decided as a boy to study art. As a young man, he traveled to London, where he studied and became an artist. He drew and painted well. He made his living through art. He was an artist until he was over forty years old.

In 1832, when he was returning from a visit to Europe, Samuel and the other passengers on his ship started talking about electricity. They liked to talk about what it might do. Morse impressed the other passengers by working out a plan for a telegraph.

Morse couldn't stop thinking about his plan. He got a little shop in New Haven, Connecticut, where he spent the next several years trying to build a telegraph. During those years he was very poor and many ridiculed him. They said that he was a fool and that he'd never build a telegraph.

However, in 1837, Samuel applied for a U.S. patent. The patent office turned him down before it finally gave him a patent because the government wasn't interested in building a telegraph line. No other country was interested, either. But the middle-aged man kept trying. On May 18, 1844, the first message was tapped out on a wire strung between Baltimore, Maryland, and Washington, D.C. The message was, "What hath God wrought!"

Congress appropriated $30,000 to build the first line. It wouldn't spend any more. Morse decided to form a private company. He wanted to spread the telegraph all over the United States. Seven years after that first message was sent, the company was formed. You know its name—Western Union.

The Answers

1. The U.S. Patent Office. _____

2. Morse applied for a patent. _____

3. He studied art there. _____

4. 1832. _____

5. Charleston, Massachusetts. _____

6. New Haven, Connecticut. _____

7. The first message sent by telegraph. _____

8. May 18, 1844. _____

Bonus Questions

A. When was the Western Union Company formed?

_____

B. How old was Morse when he first worked out his plan for the telegraph?

_____

What's the Question?

Name _____

Date _____

They once called themselves "The Roosters," and they've been together for more than thirty years. Their individual names are not well known, but their group name, The Impressions, is a big name in popular music. They've cut more than fifty records, counting remakes, and seventeen of their records have made *Billboard's* Top 40. They are Fred Cash, Sam Gooden, Ralph Johnson, and Vandy Hampton.

Their first hit, "For Your Precious Love," cut in June 1958, rose all the way to number 11. Then, during the sixties, The Impressions hit their stride. They had great group harmony and they featured low-key messages urging pride and unity among black people. "It's All Right" rose to number 4 in 1963 and "Amen" made it to number 7 in 1964. Between these two tunes were four others that made the top 20.

During the sixties, Curtis Mayfield, the pianist and guitarist, joined them and helped keep the group in the spotlight. Then Mayfield went on his own in 1969 and that nearly ended the big hits. In fact, The Impressions only cracked the top 20 once after that. Their June 1974 recording, "Finally Got Myself Together," reached number 17.

"It's hard to change your music with the times," Fred Cash said. "Music is constantly changing, and that's good. But I see our music coming back now because kids really like it. I feel that we've got a market building up."

The records sold by The Impressions total more than 20 million. Perhaps their style of music will come back.

The Answers

1. A singing group that has been together for thirty years. _____

2. "For Your Precious Love." _____

3. It made it to number 4. _____

4. He said, "Music is constantly changing . . . " _____

5. The Roosters. _____

6. Pride and unity among black people. _____

7. Fred Cash, Sam Gooden, Ralph Johnson, Vandy Hampton. _____

8. More than 20 million. _____

Bonus Questions

A. How many of The Impressions' records have not made the Top 40?

_____

B. Will the Impressions make a comeback?

                   What's the Question?